The Swindle of Innovative Educational Finance

Clare Birchall
Shareveillance: The Dangers of Openly Sharing and Covertly Collecting Data

Ian Bogost
The Geek's Chihuahua: Living with Apple

William E. Connolly
Aspirational Fascism: The Struggle for Multifaceted Democracy under Trumpism

Andrew Culp
Dark Deleuze

Sohail Daulatzai
Fifty Years of "The Battle of Algiers": Past as Prologue

Grant Farred
Martin Heidegger Saved My Life

David Golumbia
The Politics of Bitcoin: Software as Right-Wing Extremism

Gary Hall
The Uberfication of the University

John Hartigan Jr.
Aesop's Anthropology: A Multispecies Approach

Mark Jarzombek
Digital Stockholm Syndrome in the Post-Ontological Age

Nicholas A. Knouf
How Noise Matters to Finance

The Swindle of Innovative Educational Finance

Kenneth J. Saltman

University of Minnesota Press

MINNEAPOLIS

A different version of "Social Impact Bonds/Pay for Success" was previously published as "The Promise and Realities of Pay for Success/ Social Impact Bonds," *Education Policy Analysis Archives* 25 (June 2017): 59. A different version of "Student Income Loans: Transferring Wealth to Investors, Risk to Students" was previously published as "Student Income Loans Transfer Wealth to Investors, Risk to Students," truthout .org (September 2016).

Published by the University of Minnesota Press, 2018
111 Third Avenue South, Suite 290
Minneapolis, MN 55401-2520
http://www.upress.umn.edu

The University of Minnesota is an equal-opportunity educator and employer.

Contents

Introduction

THE POLITICAL RIGHT AND THE BUSINESS SECTOR in the United States have long sought to radically transform public education into a private industry. Nearly twenty years ago, *BusinessWeek* and *The Economist* described public education as a more than $600 billion opportunity ripe for the taking, comparing it to the defense, entertainment, and agriculture sectors.[1] By 2013, *Forbes* was salivating over the "Charter School Gravy Train [that] Runs Express to Fat City," even while noting the unimpressive performance of charters.[2] Valerie Strauss of the *Washington Post* explained "Why Hedge Funds Love Charter Schools."[3] It turns out it isn't the curriculum; it's the tax credits and real estate profits. By 2015, McKinsey and Company, a major force globally in promoting public school privatization and "innovative" educational finance schemes, had declared public education in the United States a $1.5 trillion sector that was growing 5 percent per year.[4] For the network of right-wing think tanks, such as Heritage, Hoover, and the American Enterprise Institute (AEI), that have steadily promoted the transformation of public education into a private industry,

1. "Reading, Writing, and Enrichment," *The Economist,* January 14, 1999; William C. Symonds, "Special Report: Education a New Push to Privatize," *Businessweek,* January 14, 2002, 11.

2. Addison Wiggin, "Charter School Gravy Train Runs Express to Fat City," *Forbes,* September 10, 2013.

3. Valerie Strauss, "Why Hedge Funds Love Charter Schools," *Washington Post,* June 4, 2014.

4. Jake Bryant and Jimmy Sarakatsannis, "Why US Education Is Ready for Investment," McKinsey & Company, July 2015, https://www.mckinsey.com/industries/social-sector/our-insights/why-us-education-is-ready-for-investment.

the big haul has long been the replacement of schools themselves with private for-profit schools or privately contracted educational services.

In several of my prior books, I have detailed the failures of corporate school reform to achieve conventional measures of academic success promised by privatization proponents, let alone to provide for critical and public forms of education.[5] I have contended that corporate profiteering in public education needs to be understood in part in terms of the broader financial uses of public education for the private sector and ruling-class people. Privatization, contracting, and commercialism represent a ruling-class pillage of the public sector for short-term gain and a change in how public education historically created profit for industry. Within the industrial economy, public education served to a great degree to reproduce the labor force by teaching knowledge and skills for work wrapped in class-based ideologies. Public education in the industrial economy largely reproduced social relations for capitalist accumulation.[6] The conditions for profit largely came from making workers with not just knowledge and skills for production but the discipline and docility to submit to production arrangements that would allow surplus labor to be extracted from the worker. In other words, public education helped set the stage for the worker to be short-changed by having her undercompensated labor contribute to the overcompensation of the owners of the production process. This industrial era swindle involved a long-term investment in making exploitable future workers. In the postindustrial economy, public schooling has increasingly become a means for

5. See, e.g., Kenneth Saltman, *The Failure of Corporate School Reform* (New York: Routledge, 2015); Saltman, *Capitalizing on Disaster: Taking and Breaking Public Schools* (New York: Routledge, 2007); Saltman, *The Edison Schools* (New York: Routledge, 2005); Saltman, *Collateral Damage* (Lanham, Md.: Rowman and Littlefield, 2000).

6. Samuel Bowles and Herbert Gintis, *Schooling in Capitalist America* (Chicago: Haymarket Books, 2011); Henry Giroux, *Theory and Resistance in Education* (Westport, Conn.: Bergin and Garvey, 1983).

capitalists to generate short-term profit through privatization, contracting, and commercialism.

While the neoliberal restructuring of public education has been steadily advancing since the 1980s, the central and most visible approaches to fully privatizing the public education system today are charter school expansion, vouchers, scholarship tax credit schemes, and "unbundling" of the school into discrete private contracted services.[7] For-profit charters allow private management companies to run schools for profit, benefiting by reducing costs and pocketing the difference between tax money and expenses. Vouchers give parents tax money to "shop" for private schooling. Scholarship tax credits or "neovouchers" incentivize parents to opt out of the public schools by funding the parents to use private schools (a significant expansion of neovouchers was packaged into the 2017 Republican tax law). Early proponents of privatizing public schooling, Chubb and Moe, along with the Hoover Institution's *Education Next Magazine,* urge citizens to abandon the very concept of the public school as outdated. Instead, citizens should embrace the consumption of private, discrete educational services. School, in this dream, looks like cable TV services. If parents want, say, art, music, or math, they will need to pay for what their children consume. Of course, part of this vision involves shifting control and ownership over schooling to technology companies where curriculum can be mass-produced, standardized, homogenized, and hence "delivered" more cheaply. While right-wing think tanks have been pushing this vision, technology companies, such as Google, Facebook/Chan Zuckerberg Initiative, Microsoft, and Apple, have moved quickly to institutionalize it.

In the United States, the big privatization schemes have recently gotten a boost with the election of Donald Trump and his appoint-

7. The concept of unbundling schooling is succinctly described by Frederick Hess, Bruno Manno, and Olivia Meeks at the American Enterprise Institute in "From School Choice to Educational Choice," http://www.aei.org/publication/from-school-choice-to-educational-choice/.

ment of longtime privatization activist Betsy Devos as secretary of education. The administration sees vouchers, for-profit charters, deregulated for-profit universities, and deregulated student lending as central to the Trump education agenda. However, there is another, far less examined dimension to educational privatization: "innovative" finance schemes. Far from being minor or secondary privatization projects, the schemes I discuss in this book represent potentially trillions of dollars of public money for the private sector to grab. Impact investing is estimated to be a $500 billion to $1 trillion sector; charter school municipal bond issuance represents a possible trillion dollar debt bubble in the making; and the privatization of higher education lending, charter school real estate investing, and commercialization of student data and personalized learning are truly massive sectors.

I began to write this book prior to Trump's election, when the terrain of educational privatization appeared slightly different. Since the 1990s, Republican *and* Democratic administrations have largely supported test-based accountability paired with privatization—especially charter school expansion. Obama's educational policy was seen by many education scholars as indistinguishable from George W. Bush's educational policy. The expected election of Hillary Clinton to the White House in 2016 promised a mildly less enthusiastic treatment of charter schools. While vouchers and scholarship tax credits would have likely made little progress, a Clinton administration would have likely seen the aggressive expansion of stealth forms of privatization packaged not through a right-wing celebration of the magic of markets but rather through a lens of efficiency, innovation, accountability, and public–private partnership. That is, it would have likely continued the new direction of educational privatization characterized by "innovative" finance schemes. Some of the most significant forms of this "innovative" educational finance are subjects of the chapters of this book: (1) social impact bonds; (2) higher educational lending privatization and student income loans; (3) charter school real estate, tax credit, and municipal bond schemes; and

(4) so-called philanthrocapitalist educational technology schemes to pass off school profiteering as charity while commercializing student data and privatizing school services through technology.

Organizationally, chapters 2–5 expose the swindles, reveal the lack of empirical evidence for them, and, more importantly, skewer the unjust values and troubling assumptions behind these schemes.

The second chapter reveals five myths that proponents use to justify social impact bonds. Social impact bonds allow banks to profit by funding social service provisions that would otherwise be directly provided by government. Banks cherry-pick already successful programs yet justify their profit taking and inflation of public service costs under the guise of measurable accountability, innovation, and corporate social responsibility.

The third chapter examines the privatization of student loan debt and the radical new form this is taking. Student income loans make students into indentured servants by tying loan repayment to future earnings. Student income loans are part of a legacy of privatizing student lending begun under the Clinton administration. Yet by transforming student loans into investment securities, they promote the vocationalization and instrumentalization of higher education.

Chapter 4 details the rise of philanthrocapitalism and its educational projects. Philanthrocapitalists like the Chan Zuckerberg Initiative, Emerson Collective, and Omidyar Network pose as philanthropies yet are actually private limited liability companies that acquire and start for-profit companies and can extract wealth with no public scrutiny, oversight, or accountability. These LLCs have moved heavily into technology-based educational contracting, personalized learning, and adaptive learning technologies and are shifting ownership and control over teaching from public school teachers to for-profit technology companies.

Chapter 5 exposes charter school real estate schemes that allow real estate investors to profit in a number of ways: by acquiring school buildings and leasing them at high rates to their own charter schools; by offering charter school municipal bonds and making charter expansion profitable by inflating a potential trillion dollar debt bubble. With a focus on charter profiteer Andre Agassi, this chapter also considers how celebrities, athletes, and musicians who largely lack educational expertise and educations themselves have come to legitimate charter-based privatization. The discussion considers how the cult of personality and a commodified image are now integral to public-sector privatization.

Regardless of which party won the White House, "innovative" educational finance as a form of privatization appears deeply entrenched in large part because the values, assumptions, and ideologies upon which it depends continue to be taught and learned, most significantly the continued propagation and post-crisis restoration of neoliberalism as both economic doctrine and cultural ideology. Not only are these innovative educational finance schemes stealth forms of educational privatization and public service privatization—forms that remain largely unknown to most citizens—but they are also promoted by investors and ideologues as falsely assuring a triumphant private-sector approach to public service provision through values of innovation, efficiency, accountability, cost savings, and, hence, responsibility. However, as the chapters that follow illustrate, these privatization schemes redistribute wealth from the public to the rich, inflate the costs of services, play accountability shell games, and function as disingenuous public relations for banks, corporations, and profiteers, suggesting that only through the profit taking of the rich can public services flourish or survive. In short, these schemes are swindles based on lies. Yet they have been legitimated by being aggressively promoted by established philanthropies like Rockefeller and Bloomberg, dominant investment banks like Goldman Sachs and Bain, democratic politicians like Deval Patrick and Rahm Emanuel, "innovative start-up" investment companies like SoFi, celebrity investors claiming their profit seeking as philanthropy like Andre Agassi and Mark Zuckerberg, and elite universities like Harvard. Another dimension that unifies these reforms is a contradiction with regard to facts, knowledge, truth, and education.

How should we make sense of the contradiction between "innovative" educational finance schemes that claim to be grounded in empirical data and numerically quantifiable measures but are in fact empirically unsupported and yet supported rather by market metaphors and faith in markets? Yes, aforementioned neoliberal ideology goes a long way in helping to explain market fundamentalism, as does the hard work of profiteers. However, there is more to explain with regard to a contemporary crisis of truth, fact, evidence, and education.

Chapter 1 sets the stage for examining the swindles of "innovative" educational finance by detailing the contemporary crisis of fact, evidence, and truth that makes the swindles possible. This contemporary crisis of fact is characterized by a contradiction in educational policy and practice between, on one hand, an endlessly espoused imperative for empirical data (data-driven teaching, data-driven leadership, data-driven policy) and, on the other hand, the pursuit of policies that are unsupported by empirical data and rely instead on market metaphors and baseless assertion of truth. This contradiction with regard to knowledge, fact, truth, and education I call the "alienation of fact." I explain this contradiction through the legacy of positivist ideology and a hostility to theory: positivism treats truth as a collection of facts that speak for themselves and do not require theory or context. The legacy of positivism makes facts appear almighty yet unmoored and estranged. This contradictory understanding of facts explains the mistaken faith in data "driving practice" in multiple fields, including policing, education, journalism, and technology. The positivist legacy represents antipathy for comprehension of how theories undergird facts, organize facts, and make facts meaningful through practices of interpretation. Facts appear omnipotent and ungrounded, a mystical inexplicable force. In such a context, theory, argumentation, and evidence are replaced by an aura of authority that is frequently grounded through reference to decontextualized numbers, essentialized bodies, institutional authority, and cults of personality. If fact comes with no theory or history, then fact appears as the result of emphatic assertion. As I discuss in the first and last chapters, this contradiction around fact and the positivist legacy explains not only the emergence of these swindles of innovative educational finance and the lie of disinterested objectivity and neutrality at the center of the testing, standards, and accountability movement in education. The alienation of fact also explains the contemporary broader crisis of truth found, for example, in the rash of conspiracy; the capacity of politicians to dismiss empirically verifiable truths as "fake news"; the problem of allegedly disinterested, objective, and neutral journalism; the authoritarian tendency of equating the authority of a truth claim with the social authority of the claimant. The alienation of fact helps explain how public-sector pillage is increasingly interwoven with the recent tendency of politics to ground assertions in numbers, bodies, and essentialized identities—false guarantees of certainty due to their association with materiality. The false guarantees of material grounding have a particular attraction when evidence, argument, and theory have been wiped out and fact appears to come from nowhere. I contend that rising material precarity amplifies the collective demand for definitive explanations just as the alienation of fact undermines people's use of knowledge for agency. As a consequence, people are turning to irrational social explanations that appear to be grounded specifically in forms that falsely promise certainty and solidity—especially numbers and bodies.

What these discussions of the ideologies of neoliberalism and positivism highlight is just how much these economic schemes are not natural developments but depend on cultural values that are produced and taught through mass media, education, policy think tanks, and other educative institutions. I hope that by exposing some of the swindles of innovative educational finance schemes, scholars, citizens, and cultural workers will oppose these stealth forms of privatization and defend democratic public spheres.

These economic schemes are undergirded by cultural and political values that are always in play, always have to be taught and learned, and hence always are subject to contestation and struggle. This project contributes to fostering cultural and political values that are less exploitative and more democratic, less extractive and more in common, less individualizing and more collective, less hierarchical and more egalitarian, less private and more public.

The Alienation of Fact: The Resurgence of Radical Empiricism in Education

THE CHAPTERS THAT FOLLOW detail innovative finance schemes that are promoted by investors through false promises of numerically quantifiable accountability, efficiency, and cost savings. These schemes represent not only swindles and lies perpetrated by rich investors intent upon getting richer, not only the culmination of decades of neoliberal ideology and corporate culture, but also a much broader crisis of truth and knowledge that extends through education, culture, and politics.

This chapter explains the central role of radical empiricism and the hostility to theory in education and journalism in the contemporary crisis of truth and knowledge that underlies the swindle of innovative educational finance. In the contemporary crisis of truth, in place of theory, argument, and evidence, people are seeking foundations for assertion in forms that offer a false promise of certainty—numbers and bodies. My discussion focuses on the contradiction between the simultaneous faith in fact for public, academic, and policy discourse and yet the widespread disregard for fact, evidence, argument, and truth in these domains. The first sections take up this contradiction in education historically and at present. The second part addresses journalism, and the third discusses how both can be understood as the alienation of fact, the replacement of fact with dogma. This problem of knowledge, evidence, and fact is driving a dangerous turn toward not just decontextualized numbers and a frenzy for empty displays of efficacy to ground assertion but, worse yet, essentialized identitarian forms of politics that seek to ground truth in allegedly good and bad bodies. As I explain, the crisis of truth, fact, evidence, and theory is profoundly wrapped up with the recent resurgence of white supremacy, anti-Semitism, xenophobia, and sexism as well as rampant conspiracy and political authoritarianism. As Zygmunt Bauman contends, material precarity produced through growing inequality and the upward amassing of wealth drives people to seek security in the Strongman.[1] My argument here is that the estrangement of fact compels a similar frenzied pursuit of security in the false promise of material grounding found in numbers and bodies.

Across social institutions, an imperative for positivism demands data accumulation, data display, data-driven leadership, and data-driven accountability regimes. In the tradition of positivist rationality, facts are alienated from the conditions of their production and appear to speak for themselves, to be meaningful on their own, requiring no interpretation.

A number of fields have succumbed to "data-driven" rhetoric. Police departments use CompStat to aggregate and crunch crime statistics and then orient their policing activities to "juke the stats." Journalism remains bound to the guise of disinterested objectivity. Perhaps more than any other field, the imperative for positivism pervades education. Public schooling uses test-based accountability in which learning is equated with numerical test scores and changes to teaching and administrative practice are to be guided by the numerical outcomes. Superintendents, principals, and teachers are, according to educational rhetoric and doxa, to be driven not by theorizing educational situations but rather by data. "Data-driven" discourse presumes that the data are not collected with underlying theoretical assumptions or interpreted with theoretical assumptions.

All of the major recent educational policies, such as the revised teacher education accreditation body Council for the

---

1. Zygmunt Bauman, *Strangers at Our Door* (New York: Polity, 2016).

Accreditation of Educator Preparation, formerly the National Council for Accreditation of Teacher Education, the Pearson-run student teaching assessment platform edTPA, and the Common Core State Standards, have underlying assumptions. These policies assume that knowledge is a deliverable commodity, that teachers are delivery agents, and that students are knowledge consumers. These policies share an approach to learning and knowledge characterized by an active denial of how knowledge relates to the experience and subjectivity of students and teachers. As well, these policies refuse to take into account how learning and knowledge relate to the world and the capacity of subjects to use knowledge to shape it. That is, dominant educational policies presume a conception of agency in which the social power of the individual derives from the acquisition and exchange of socially consecrated knowledge. Agency in this view does not stem from the use of knowledge to interpret, judge, act on, and shape the social world while reflecting on what one does. Instead, agency appears as consumption and display of knowledge for academic promotion and later material consumption.

Similarly, value-added modeling calls for K–12 administrators to measure teacher performance by standardized test outputs and links compensation and job security to the numbers. Universities defund the interpretive humanities and expand fields not just with commercial application but also with empirical orientation, while theory is replaced by a renewed archival research and emphasis on data collection. Higher education is regularly being subject to calls for quantifying student learning through tests and then tying financing to the outputs. Student income loans make this explicit as private tuition lending is tied to the expected future earnings of the student. Similarly, the Department of Education under Obama began measuring the value of universities based on the future earnings of students relative to the costs of the education. Of course, these projects not only belie an instrumental rationality in which interpretive forms of learning have no place but also lend themselves to being linked to commercial exchange and commercial competition.

The expansion of radical empiricism coincides with a crisis of truth, evidence, knowledge, information, and education. This crisis of truth appears in educational discourse as particularly market-based educational policy and practices are promoted and implemented regardless of a lack of evidence for them or even despite counterevidence. For example, vouchers, charters, school turnarounds, and urban portfolio models are all privatization schemes that are either unsupported by empirical evidence or undermined by empirical evidence, or for which empirical evidence are impossible to obtain.[2] Nonetheless, all of these schemes are promoted by rightist think tanks. The Department of Education under both parties has embraced unsubstantiated policies swayed by advocacy organizations. Both conservative and liberal think tanks largely remain with the radical empiricist model, bickering back and forth in policy briefs over numbers and measurement methodologies and seldom going beyond disputes over efficacy. Do, for example, charter schools slightly raise or slightly lower very low test scores in schools in urban and rural poverty? Such an empirical question displaces scrutiny of how schooling is implicated in the reproduction of radical economic inequality not only through the unequal distribution of educational resources but through the unequal distribution of cultural capital. The focus on positivist measures of numerical efficacy elides questions about and contests over the economic, political, and cultural purposes and roles of schooling. Implicit in the efficacy debates is an assumption that schools assimilate people for the existing social order rather than seeing schools as a site and stake of struggle to imagine and enact a freer, more equal, and more just society.

2. Three major new studies of vouchers were released at the start of 2017 that joined with other studies and international studies from Chile and India to paint an utterly damning picture of the empirical case for vouchers. See Martin Carnoy, "School Vouchers Are Not a Proven Strategy for Improving Student Achievement," Economic Policy Institute, February 28, 2017, http://www.epi.org/publication/school-vouchers-are-not-a-proven-strategy-for-improving-student-achievement/.

The Legacy of Radical Empiricism in Education

The practices of K–12 schooling and the field of education have a long history with radical empiricism. Empiricist theories of learning date back to Locke and Rousseau with a conception of the student as an empty vessel needing to be filled with knowledge or as a blank slate to be written upon. While August Compte conceived of positivism in the nineteenth century, it was not until the early twentieth century that positivist models of teaching and learning were developed from the ideals of industrial efficiency and Frederick Taylor's scientific management. The school was reconceptualized as a factory. Across the United States, the Gary Plan was implemented, according to which the time and space of school were organized to model a factory with shifts and bells. Knowledge was imagined as an industrial product that needed to be ever more efficiently produced and transmitted and to be consumed by the student. Teachers' work within this view ought to be seen like factory work and could be broken down and made more efficient, sped up, and measured. From the 1930s to the 1960s, scientific management surged in education. It was bolstered by the rise of educational psychology and its eugenic legacy that sought to establish an empirical science of intelligence, learning, and ability.[3] The eugenics legacy of testing and standardization of knowledge and the learning process merged with the industrial manufacturing promotion of standardization of knowledge as product and process needing to be made ever more efficient.

In the 1970s and 1980s, a growing body of liberal and radical educational scholarship pushed back against radical empiricism. This literature drew on the earlier progressive and radical educational theory of Dewey and George Counts. Social and cultur-

---

3. See, e.g., Stephen Jay Gould's *The Mismeasure of Man* (New York: W. W. Norton, 1996) or a contemporary dissection of the application of these ideas in Mark Garrison, *A Measure of Failure* (Albany: State University of New York Press, 2009).

al reproduction theorists and proponents of critical pedagogy also appropriated from Marx, Gramsci, the Frankfurt School of Critical Theory, and critical sociology as well as from feminist theory, pragmatism, black studies, and poststructuralism. Unlike the dominant positivist discourses, radical education theory emphasized the inherently political nature of teaching and learning, the politics of knowledge and curriculum, and the assumption that all educational practices are undergirded by theories whether recognized or not. Against the assumption of a universally valuable and disinterested view of schooling, radical educational theorists drew on Gramsci to emphasize the extent to which the school and the curriculum are sites and stakes of class and cultural struggle. Against the positivist view of the subject as a receptacle for commodified units of knowledge, radical education theory, such as that of Paulo Freire and Henry Giroux, emphasized that theory is always behind educational practices and that the question is really whether teachers are aware of the theories that they employ.[4] Radical educators pushed back against the tendency of psychological and developmental radical empiricist approaches to biologize, naturalize, and individualize educational practices. Instead, they emphasized the social, political, and cultural aspects of pedagogy and curriculum. Against reformist tinkering and empirical efficacy debates, radical educators emphasized the radically democratic potential of schooling to foster critical consciousness and political agency by making acts of interpretation the basis for acts of social intervention and collective self governance.

While critical educational studies drew on a broad array of critical theories in the social sciences and the humanities, the majority of subdisciplines in education in the latter half of the twentieth century were predominantly influenced by empirical psychology. In the late 1990s, economics became the dominant

---

4. See Paulo Freire, *Pedagogy of the Oppressed* (New York: Continuum, 1972), and Giroux, *Theory and Resistance in Education*.

trope through which educational studies were framed. The dominance of economic framings of educational problems and solutions from the 1980s to the present owes in no small part to the expansion of neoliberal ideology in education and the related accountability movement.

From the 1980s to the present, radical empiricism has played a central role in the radical restructuring of public education by bringing together two key trends: (1) neoliberal privatization in its various forms paired with (2) the radically empiricist accountability and standards movement. Neoliberal privatization involved public-sector defunding, privatizations like charters and vouchers, commercialism, managerialism, and the ideology of corporate culture. The accountability and standards movement involves heavy standardized testing; high-stakes testing in which funding depends on raised test scores; standardization of curriculum; and the expansion of technologies for tracking, testing, and homogenizing. Privatization and accountability are two mutually reinforcing trends with radical empiricism at their centers. Neoliberal privatization has been justified since the early 1980s by incessant declarations of the failure of public education. Such declared failure has been framed through the register of market and military competition, but it has drawn most heavily on selective claims as to numerical standardized test score failures. Test-based failures have been claimed through reference to international and domestic comparisons such as the Organisation for Economic Cooperation and Development's PISA scores as well as to the low test scores of urban schools.[5] Public school failure declarations erase how the tests represent the class position of students, their cultural capital, and the radically different histories of investment in schools and communities. Working-class and poor schools that

5. See David Berliner and Bruce Biddle, *The Manufactured Crisis* (New York: Basic Books, 1996), and, more recently, Gene Glass and David Berliner, *50 Myths and Lies that Threaten America's Public Schools: The Real Crisis in Education* (New York: Teachers College Press, 2014).

were deemed to have "failed" in part through reference to the scores were considered ripe for experimentation, especially with the market. Hence urban and rural poor schools were targeted for privatization in the form of chartering, vouchers, for-profit contracting, and corporate managerial reforms.

The accountability and standards movement has itself been a massive for-profit industry in test, textbook, and electronic curricular products. The standardization of curriculum has been promoted as allowing greater control over the delivery and consumption of knowledge. Standardized testing and prescriptive standardized curriculum products have come to dominate public school curriculum. Standardized tests erase the process of knowledge making by disappearing the people who make the tests as well as their social positions, interests, theoretical assumptions, and ideological commitments. Facts in this view come from nowhere, are delivered, and are either properly or improperly consumed. As standardized tests disappear from view those real people who deem particular knowledge valuable, they frame knowledge as being grounded by institutional authority rather than good arguments with solid evidence. Standardized tests also evacuate the necessary act of interpretation of fact that is foreclosed by the prescribed choices of four or five possible answers. Such practices make learning seem mechanical, as though one collects little pieces of knowledge along a path that is there before one encounters it. Such practices also obscure the politics of knowledge—that knowledge is contested and that contests over claims to truth are linked to broader material and symbolic interests and social positions. They falsely universalize knowledge that is partial and that represents ruling groups. Standardized testing practices actively displace the possibility of critical pedagogical practices that draw on theory to make central to teaching and learning investigation of the relationships between knowledge and power. Contrary to standardized testing, which emphasizes consumption of decontextualized fact and monological depositing of knowledge, critical pedagogical practices foster knowledge making through dialogue to create the conditions to comprehend and act on the self and society.

Venture philanthropists like Gates and Broad have spent millions to promote educational administration and leadership that are "data driven." They have funded database tracking projects that aim to align numerical measures of test performance to behaviors and then use the data to inform and control behaviors of teachers. More recently, as I discuss in chapter 4, philanthrocapitalists like the Chan Zuckerberg Initiative (CZI) and major technology companies are promoting the replacement of teachers and dialogic forms of learning with mass-produced corporate knowledge products that can be quantified and standardized. In this case, the disregard for the specificities of subjectivity and context is sold as their opposite. As I discuss in my recent book *Scripted Bodies,* a number of radically empiricist projects now pair positivism with control of bodies. For example, nootropic drugs or smart drugs, typically amphetamines, are used to drug kids into attention for standardized test performance or to drug kids into controlling themselves so as not to disturb other kids' testing. Grit pedagogy revives behaviorism through tactics for learned bodily self-control—a new corporeally targeted neoliberal character education. In the tradition of positivism, the dominant educational reforms presume that knowledge and learning are delinked from both the experience of the learning subject and the broader social world.

So, on one hand, educational policy and practice have become thoroughly dominated by the assumption that what matter most are just the facts. On the other hand, there is an incredible disregard for facts, information, evidence, or reasoned argument when it comes to the most dominant educational policy pushes. For example, Donald Trump's secretary of education Betsy Devos spent twenty years promoting educational privatization in Michigan. Devos promoted for-profit chartering and vouchers. Both policies have an empirical record of poor performance in test-based achievement.[6] However, there is a long legacy of right-wing promotion of failed market-based reform. There is a long empirical record of the disaster of vouchers internationally—a record of gutting the public education system; of vastly exacerbating unequal-quality schools; and of causing the proliferation of cheap, bad, for-profit schools for the poor.[7] Vouchers in the United States have long been promoted as a way to get a foot in the door for educational privatization. Once a single market-based scheme can be launched, then right-wing think tanks can call for more studies and more experiments.

Another clear case in point of a complete disregard for evidence is the right-wing promotion of charter schooling as a catalyst to replace public schooling with a private industry. Andy Smarick in the Hoover Institution's magazine *Education Next* was quite explicit that the right should champion charters in the short run to justify declaration of charters as a public failed experiment and to justify more widespread privatization.[8] Paul T. Hill, like Smarick, calls for "churn" or "creative destruction." Hill, of the neoliberal Center for Reinventing Public Education, relentlessly promoted "urban portfolio districts" to expand charter-based privatization and admitted in his advocacy work that there would be no way to empirically ascertain whether the urban portfolio model of "churn," opening and closing schools and chartering, would result in improvements in academic performance.[9] However, Hill insist-

6. Caitlin Emma, Benjamin Wermund, and Kimberly Hefling, "Devos' Michigan Schools Experiment Gets Poor Grades," *Politico,* http://www.politico.com/story/2016/12/betsy-devos-michigan-school-experiment-232399. For a review of the educational policy scholarship situated in terms of a broader advocacy of critical education, see Saltman, *Failure of Corporate School Reform.*

7. Carnoy, "School Vouchers."

8. Andy Smarick, "The Turnaround Fallacy: Stop Trying to Fix Failing Schools. Close Them and Start Fresh," *Education Next* 10, no. 1 (2010), http://educationnext.org/the-turnaround-fallacy/.

9. Paul T. Hill, with Christine Campbell et al., *Portfolio School Districts for Big Cities: An Interim Report* (Seattle, Wash.: Center on Reinventing

ed that the privatizations afforded by the model justify it. Smarick, Hill, and other market fundamentalists aim to replace public education with a private, for-profit industry in education.

The thinking of such ideologues was behind the radical privatization of public education in New Orleans after Hurricane Katrina and in Chicago following the razing of its public housing projects. Following the storm, the New Orleans public schools and the teachers' union were dismantled and replaced by a network of four charter districts. Chicago closed a significant portion of its neighborhood public schools and replaced them with charters. Recently, scholars like Sean Reardon at Stanford and journalists like David Leonhardt of the *New York Times* have promoted claims that New Orleans and Chicago represent evidence of school improvement following radical neoliberal restructuring (school closures, privatizations, and union busting), pointing to small increases in standardized test scores.[10] While New Orleans by 2017 saw a three-year decline in test scores, most studies of Chicago charters find nearly identical test scores as neighborhood schools. Meanwhile, those making these claims of improvement are being sure to ignore the massive displacement of working-class and poor students and families from these cities combined with rising family incomes. Standardized tests consistently correlate with family income.[11] Following Katrina in New Orleans, the poorest families were dispossessed of their communities. The four new charter districts represent a different population than the one prior to the storm. Similarly, following massive planned gentrification/pub-

Public Education, October 2009); Saltman, *Failure of Corporate School Reform.*

10. David Leonhardt, "A Plea for a Fact-Based Debate about Charter Schools," *New York Times,* July 22, 2018; Sean F. Reardon and Rebecca Hinze-Pifer, *Test Score Growth among Chicago Public School Students, 2009–2014* (Stanford, Calif.: Stanford Center for Education Policy Analysis, November 2017).

11. See the National Assessment of Educational Progress, https://www.nationsreportcard.gov/.

lic housing and neighborhood school closure coordinated by the Commercial Club of Chicago and more than a decade of steadily rising family income in the city, the tests are measuring different students and, most importantly, richer students. As sociologist Pierre Bourdieu explained, test scores correlate to family income because the tests measure the knowledge, tastes, and dispositions of professional and ruling-class people, who also happen to be the ones who commission and make the tests. So what appears to be happening is a situation where rich investors are pushing the poorest people out of cities, putting in place market-based school reforms, testing the new population, and claiming that it was the reforms rather than the dispossession that caused the alleged change. These selective empirical studies that aim to use numbers to settle the question of neoliberal educational restructuring raise more questions than answers. Did the tests go up or down? Are these the same or different students? Ultimately, these narrow questions miss the point that the privatization agenda has no way of addressing the brutal inequalities between those living in the rich and poor parts of these cities or the ways that schools organized around standardization, testing, and privatization exacerbate and legitimize such inequality rather than challenging it. The ideologues not only misrepresent positivist standardized tests as definitive evidence of meaningful learning but also fail to account for epidemic cases of charters pushing out the students who are the hardest to educate, including those needing special education, English language learners, and those identified as discipline problems. These claims of neoliberal restructuring working are examples of ideological uses of evidence for justifying a privatization agenda.

Mark Fisher described in his book *Capitalist Realism* this fictive performance of quantifiable efficacy as "market Stalinism." The contradiction between the imperative for radical empiricist approaches to policy and practice and the abandonment of evidence and argumentation is playing out in media culture, more specifically, in news and journalism.

Fake News, Journalism, and the Evacuation of Theory

Following the election of Donald Trump, numerous essays in the popular press have offered explanations for how a flagrant and compulsive liar with no regard for truth or evidence could garner widespread support. Although many politicians lie, the quantity and brazenness of Trump's lies represent broader disregard for empirical evidence and for education. As of August 4, 2018 (not that anybody's counting, but . . .), Trump publicly lied or made misleading statements 4,229 times.[12] Examples of the disregard for evidence range from insisting that Obama was not born in the United States to rejecting the scientific consensus about human-caused climate change, scapegoating undocumented immigrants by accusing them of rape and murder, making impossible claims about financing a border wall, describing his loss of the popular vote as winning by a landslide, and nominating figures like Mike Flynn to head the National Security Agency (Flynn falsely claims that Sharia law is being built in the United States, and his reputation for untruth got his statements derided in the military as "Flynn Facts"). Examples of his disregard for education include stating that he "likes the uneducated" to appointing education secretary Betsy Devos, who remains committed to expanding vouchers and for-profit charter schooling even as her efforts in Michigan have resulted in overwhelming empirical evidence that these policies worsen schools and lower test scores.[13] Devos has also financially supported organizations dedicated to expanding the use of public money for private religious education. As Devos's nomination moved forward, additional statements and actions

12. Fact Checker, "President Trump Has Made 4,229 False or Misleading Claims in 558 Days," *Washington Post,* August 4, 2018, https://www.washingtonpost.com/news/fact-checker/wp/2018/08/01/president-trump-has-made-4229-false-or-misleading-claims-in-558-days/?utm_term=.49e4aee342c8.

13. Emma et al., "Devos' Michigan Schools Experiment."

raised questions as to her commitment to truth, fact, and evidence. These ranged from defending guns in schools to protect against grizzly bears, as she stated in her Senate confirmation hearing, to her investments in a sham brain treatment center that shows children with autism and ADHD movies and interrupts them when they stop paying attention.[14] In fact, getting more guns in schools does not make schools safer: guns appear not to be the best defense against the scourge of grizzlies (pepper spray does work). There is no empirical evidence either for the movie-based brain treatments.

Popular press explanations for the acceptability and even widespread embrace of untruth include varieties of "blame the internet." One version of "blame the internet" offers the "fake news" narrative in which the abundance of ersatz news stories rendered the population incapable of distinguishing real from fake news. The stories about "fake news" imply that "real news" could allow citizens to make informed choices, just as such "real news" covered the 2016 election with nearly no investigative journalism or dissection of the untruths spoken by politicians, let alone minimal analysis of policy proposals. However, "real news" suffers from saturation by commercial promotional content.

Media theorist Robert McChesney has demonstrated that the decline of investigative journalism must be understood as the result of corporate media consolidation rather than internet competition for news outlets.[15] The decline of investigative journalism has resulted in news content consisting of about 90 percent public relations content. As corporate media venues covered fake news and its role in the election, right-wing media outlets propelled

14. Ulrich Boser, "Betsy Devos Has Invested Millions in This Brain Training Center. So I Checked It Out," *Washington Post,* May 26, 2017, https://www.washingtonpost.com/posteverything/wp/2017/05/26/betsy -devos-neurocore/?utm_term=.366a865e3c3d.

15. See Robert McChesney, *Digital Disconnect* (New York: The New Press, 2013).

by Trump's claims began characterizing mainstream media news itself as fake news. Outlandish fake news stories were generated to drive internet click-through profits, especially during the 2016 presidential election. Web entrepreneurs wrote sensational stories, such as one about Hillary Clinton operating a pedophile prostitution ring out of a pizza parlor: "Pizzagate." An armed vigilante intent on saving the victims fired his rifle in the restaurant, only to discover that Hillary Clinton and the children she was pimping were not there.

The problem of the news media involves not only the extent to which content production has been compromised by commerce but also the extent to which educative institutions have failed to provide citizens with the tools to interpret the quality of sources and veracity of claims. For example, most Americans have not learned about the standards and varieties of editorial review, such as journalistic and scholarly review and the differences between these and an internet posting. Functional literacy now requires the capacity to distinguish sources of information lest we all heroically invade pedophile prostitution pizza parlors. Yet functional literacy is not enough.

One crucial element missing from the discussion of fake news is the way that both professional journalism and fake news disavow the politics of knowledge behind claims to truth. Mainstream journalism effaces its own framing assumptions and theoretical presuppositions behind the framing of narratives, the collection of facts, and the interpretation of the meaning of those facts. Rightist critics of media began describing mainstream journalism as fake news, alleging that mainstream journalism is a collection of false facts rather than criticizing the values, assumptions, and positions that underlie the narratives. Following allegations that fake news was involved in Trump's election, Trump himself declared CNN "fake news," and he has been repeating and expanding this accusation. Trump got this right, but for the wrong reasons. CNN's problem most of the time is not ludicrous, made-up stories but rather the failure to provide examination of competing values, assumptions, and ideologies behind claims to truth as well as the relationship between these symbolic contests and material ones. The lie built into mainstream media is the guise of disinterested objectivity in which ruling-class and dominant cultural group interests are obscured and universalized, as the *New York Times* motto puts it, as "All the News that's Fit to Print." Corporate media juxtapose falsehoods in the fake news with their own allegedly disinterested and neutral "true" news coverage. The missing element from both perspectives is consideration of the theory behind the organization and interpretation of fact. The lie of disinterested objectivity is the same lie built into standardized tests and curriculum.

Another popular press explanation for the crisis of truth has to do with the nature of the Trump supporters. Rebecca McWilliams, writing in *The Nation* magazine, provides the "Hunter Thompson Hell's Angel's revenge theory" of the angry white working-class male.[16] In this explanation for the affirmation of untruth by the electorate, decades of alienation driven by neoliberal globalization have resulted in an economically and politically excluded population of white men who are driven primarily by revenge against political and educated elites. In this narrative, Trump's rejection of fact, evidence, and truth is not a problem for supporters because they are well aware that politics is a show and, most importantly, believe that Donald Trump the showman will stick it to elites (of course, after the election, he proceeded to stock the government with Wall Street and billionaire elites). This perspective suggests that the real promise of Trump was one of subverting the elite establishment. In fact, the more transgressive Trump's statements became, the more credence they gave to the perception that he was a true threat to the ruling establishment and not beholden to the rules of a game that elites had rigged against most of the population. Hence Trump provided a point of identification for

16. Susan McWilliams, "This Political Theorist Predicted the Rise of Trumpism: His Name Was Hunter S. Thompson," *The Nation,* December 15, 2016.

citizens in which his lies were a catalyst to a greater truth that the mainstream media, political class, academics, and economic elites largely didn't want to admit—that an ostensibly fair system is in fact a system rigged by and for elites at the expense of most. Like critical theorists, the Trump voter is deeply suspicious of appearances. However, the critical theorist wants to take experience, appearance, and claims to truth on a detour through theory.

Theory provides an examination of the values, assumptions, and ideologies that undergird claims to truth. It allows facts to be interpreted and situated in terms of broader structural and systemic patterns, history, and context. Theory also allows one to comprehend how the interpretive scaffold of the subject is formed by the social and how the social is formed of subjects. Theory allows one to reflect on one's actions, and it expands the language to mediate experience and interpret facts. Theory expands political agency, and political agency is crucial for a democratic society.

The Trump voter employs conspiracy rather than theory. Conspiracy imagines that there are superagents endowed with the ability to secretly determine outcomes. Within the logic of conspiracy, those on the outside of the conspiracy are left with spectatorial agency—able to get a glimpse of the conspiracy but without the tools to make sense of what produced a particular social phenomenon or experience. Bad superagents, the conspirators, conspire to conceal fact, propagate lies, and shape history in the shadows. Only good superagents who allegedly embody truth, such as a charismatic and strong leader, can reveal the conspiracy (that is, fabricate it) and then shape history on behalf of the victims of the conspirators. The conspirators, on the other hand, do not simply speak untruth; they embody untruth. The problem for the Nazis wasn't that the Jews believed the wrong thing and needed to be reeducated to the right views. It was who they were, their essence, their nature. The problem for Trump and the alt-right is not radical Islam but Muslims themselves—hence the ban on travel from Muslim-majority countries under the pretext of security, despite the fact that there had been no terrorist attacks by individuals of those nations since before September 11. For conspiracy, the identity-based grounding of the enemy is not a coincidence but rather consistent with the need to give a material grounding to anchor the accusation. The body functions like numbers in the world of alienated fact, providing an aura of foundation to scapegoating and lies.

From vaccines causing autism to fluoride in drinking water, birtherism, chemtrails to 9/11 conspiracy, Holocaust denial, QAnon, and so on, a frenzy of irrationalism belies a deep distrust of facts and yet a faith in fact unmoored from the history and context that gives fact its meaning. In a culture in which positivism suggests the supremacy of the fact, fact is decontextualized and dehistoricized, appearing to come from nowhere—to be all powerful and yet deeply suspicious. In such a context, the repetition of baseless assertion and lies flourishes.

Another popular explanation for the embrace of untruth could be called the "mainstreaming of postmodernism" position. This view suggests that we are now living in a "posttruth" era in which most people recognize that uncertainties about facts, spin, or partial narratives are the new norm. Such a view could be seen in popular discourse when George W. Bush's chief of staff, Karl Rove, derided journalists in the "reality-based community" who criticized the president for ignoring reality. Rove claimed that, by acting, those in power make a new reality. Stephen Colbert named the tendency to ignore facts in making assertions "truthiness." Oil and tobacco companies have long embraced postmodern truth by hiding their own empirical studies of lung cancer and human-caused climate change and insisting that there are a multitude of competing narratives and bodies of evidence and hence these dangers cannot be grounded. In the absence of definitive proof, let's keep burning fossils and cigarettes. Critics of this mainstreaming of postmodern truth view refer to the material limits of epistemological uncertainty. Facts matter like the fact of gravity when jumping out of a window. However, Trump's open and irrational rejection of empirical evidence is very different from antifoundationalism in its pragmatist, postmodern, or critical theory forms, in which competing narratives, arguments, and evidence call into question the possibility of access to certain knowledge of objective reality. As in science, these positions share a comfort with truth being provisional, antifoundational, and fallible and with the best theoretical assumptions, arguments, and evidence winning until better ones can displace them.

The Alienation of Fact

How do we make sense of this glaring contradiction between, on one hand, the imperative for positivism in which the fact is positioned as the supreme self-evident value and, on the other hand, the abandonment of fact, evidence, or even truth itself when it comes to speech and policy? What explain these contradictions playing out in both educational and media discourse are (1) the alienation of fact and (2) the related replacement of reasoned argument with faith/dogma.

Critical theory has a long tradition of analyzing how dogma sediments in social consciousness. German social theorist Theodor Adorno, for example, drew on the sociological analysis of George Simmel to offer an explanation for the allure of positivism. Adorno explained that in a capitalist world in which everything is for sale, everything loses its value other than as a means of abstract exchange.[17] This loss of value renders all things abstract, and everything in the social world is experienced as floating and ephemeral. Numbers promise to restore the solidity and certainty lost through alienation. We can think about this with regard to standardized testing. Standardized testing has now been dominating public education for nearly twenty years, since No Child Left Behind was launched in 2001. Knowledge is decontextualized and truth claims are delinked from their conditions of production in the standard-

17. Theodor Adorno, *Introduction to Sociology* (Stanford, Calif.: Stanford University Press, 2002).

ized test. That is, by disappearing those who make claims to truth, their interests, and social and ideological positions, standardized tests ground knowledge claims in the institutional authority of the test. Yet the attachment of numbers to the test performance provides a scientistic aura of certainty that recontextualizes knowledge and the test taker within a system of educational exchange that leads through academic promotion to a promise ultimately of economic exchange. The attachment of numbers to truth claims and their false promise of certainty and solidity has resulted in a now dominant way of thinking about learning as earning.

Numerical quantification applies not science but a guise of science or scientism, invoking a careful and systematic process of measurement. It also suggests disinterestedness, objectivity, and universality. It provides a feeling of control by invoking abstract objectivity and universality. While numbering things offers a response to the alienation of market exchange everywhere, it is also alienating in its tendency to delimit the relationship between subjectivity and the objective world.

To extend Adorno's insight, we might consider those activities to which the attachment of numerical quantification is anathema. Numbers do not promise certainty and solidity in certain contexts. Think about your closest relationships, the people you care most about. Imagine those you love providing a numerical rating for your affections. "Dinner with you was an 8.5." Imagine telling a joke with a friend and getting a numerical rating in return. What these examples highlight is that our pleasures for human intimacy and intersubjective connection are contrary to the promise of numerical control offered by positivism. Quantification as a remedy for alienation simultaneously offers a guise of control while creating more alienation. Those suffering from obsessive-compulsive disorder (OCD) often have a need to apply numerical rituals to experiences. For example, to leave a room, someone with OCD may need to open and close the door a certain number of times or count the number of steps to the door. The counting provides a temporary feeling of control otherwise experienced as lacking in these individuals. The numbers do not fix the obsession; they just briefly soothe the anxiety. Is not the ideology of positivism a kind of collective OCD offering a soothing yet false promise of control over a physical world experienced as slipping away, as melting in air? The alienation of fact involves the disappearance of the conditions of production of fact, the mystification of fact, and the treatment of fact as dogma to be transmitted and received.

What stands behind the absence of evidence and reasoned argument in educational policy and practice is faith—a faith in markets. The faith in markets is not only the result of decades of neoliberal ideology and the promotion of the there is no alternative (to the market; TINA) thesis but also of decades of schooling in which knowledge has been positioned as true by virtue of the authority of the claimant. The era of standardized testing has effectively accomplished this equation of truth with authority by alienating truth claims, making them appear to come from nowhere and having authority by virtue of their anonymous authorship. Standardized tests do not come with the tools to question or dispute; they defy dialogue and follow the logic of monologue.

In my book *The Failure of Corporate School Reform,* I discussed the relationship between the new uses of positivism in education and market fundamentalism or capitalist dogma. What I termed the new market positivism is typified by the reinvigorated expansion of long-standing positivist approaches to schooling: standardized testing, standardization of curriculum, the demand for policy grounded exclusively in allegedly scientific (really scientistic) empirically based pedagogical reforms, the drumbeat against educational theory and in favor of practicalism. The new market positivism signals the use of these long-standing approaches toward the expansion of multiple forms of educational privatization.

In the Fordist era, positivism neutralized, naturalized, and universalized social and cultural reproduction under the guise of the public good, the public interest, but also individual values of humanist education. Critical educational scholars of the 1970s and 1980s referred to this obscuring of the capitalist reproduction function of the public school as the "hidden curriculum." The economic role of schooling as a sorting and sifting mechanism for the capitalist economy was largely denied. As Pierre Bourdieu and Jean Passeron pointed out, mechanisms such as testing simultaneously stratify based on class while *concealing* how merit and talent stand in for the unequal distribution of life chances.[18] Reproduction in the new market positivism still neutralizes and naturalizes the unequal distribution of life chances through the unequal distribution of cultural and social capital. Class mobility in the United States is far less possible today. But the new market positivism also openly naturalizes and universalizes a particular economic basis for all educational relationships while justifying a shift in governance and control over educational institutions. Testing, database projects designed to boil down the allegedly most efficient knowledge delivery systems and reward and punish teachers and students—these are not only at the center of pedagogical, curricular, and administrative reform but also are openly justified through the allegedly universal benefits of capitalism. The new market positivism subjects all to standardization and normalization of knowledge, denying the class and cultural interests, the political struggle behind the organization and framing of claims to truth. The new market positivism links its denial and concealment of the politics of knowledge to its open and aggressive application of capitalist ideology, that is, the faith in the religion of capitalism, to every aspect of public schooling.

In *Escape from Freedom,* Erich Fromm suggests that the very possibility of modern rationality comes from disobedience, dislocation, and estrangement. The child's "no" introduces a separation from parental authority. For Fromm, the social and historical conditions for self-reflection come from the alienating effects of capitalism. Only by being estranged from the land and labor and from

18. Pierre Bourdieu and Jean Passeron, *Reproduction in Education Society and Culture* (Thousand Oaks, Calif.: Sage, 1990).

social relations can one make an object of analysis of oneself and society. Paulo Freire, Henry Giroux, and others followed Fromm's thought in advocating the making of both subjective experience and analysis of the objective social world objects of critical analysis. In the tradition of critical pedagogy, the process of theorizing self and society creates the conditions for humanization and agency by countering capitalist objectification in its many forms.

As both liberals and conservatives continue to embrace positivist forms of education and journalism, they contribute to the alienation of fact and the crisis of truth it makes. Against the "bad alienation of fact" of radical empiricism that decontextualizes and dehistoricizes truth claims, critical pedagogy puts forward what we could call a "good alienation of fact" that seeks to contextualize and comprehend not only the theoretical assumptions and ideological underpinnings but also the broader material interests, social forces, and symbolic contests that are imbricated with claims to truth. Critical pedagogy estranges experience and truth claims by denaturalizing them and treating them as an object of analysis. Critical pedagogy reinvests claims to truth with the conditions of their production—that is, the history, context, and social contests that give truth claims meaning. It provides an approach to knowledge that emphasizes how acts of interpretation of fact can form the basis for social intervention. Critical pedagogy fosters democratic dispositions, including linking the process of learning to engagement with public problems and the commitment to dialogic forms of learning and public life. As such, critical pedagogy asserts the potential for fact, when theorized and interpreted, to be a source of agency rather than an oppressive, alienated force.

Social Impact Bonds/Pay for Success

INVESTMENT BANKS such as Goldman Sachs, Bank of America, and J. P. Morgan; philanthropies such as the Rockefeller Foundation; politicians such as Chicago Mayor Rahm Emanuel and Massachusetts former governor and now Bain Capital managing director Deval Patrick; and elite universities such as Harvard have been aggressively promoting Pay for Success (also known as social impact bonds) as a solution to intractable financial and political problems facing public education and other public services. In these schemes, investment banks pay for public services to be contracted out to private providers and stand to earn much more money than the cost of the service. For example, Goldman Sachs put up $16.6 million to fund an early childhood education program in Chicago, yet it is getting more than $30 million[1] from the city. While Pay for Success is only at its early stages in the United States, the Rockefeller Foundation and Merrill Lynch estimate that by 2020, the market size for impact investing will reach between $400 billion and $1 trillion.[2] The Every Student Succeeds Act of 2016, the latest iteration of the Elementary and Secondary Education Act of 1965, directs federal dollars to incentivize these for-profit educational endeavors significantly, legitimizing and institutionalizing them.

1. Melissa Sanchez, "Investors Earn Max Initial Payment from Chicago's 'Social Impact Bond,'" *Chicago Reporter,* May 16, 2016, https://www.chicagoreporter.com/investors-earn-max-initial-payment-from-chicagos-social-impact-bond/.
2. Sophie Quinton, "How Goldman Sachs Can Help Save the Safety Net," *National Journal,* May 10, 2013, 1.

Pay for Success is promoted by proponents as an innovative financing technique that brings together social service providers with private funders and nonprofit organizations committed to expanding social service provision. In theory, Pay for Success expands accountability because programs are independently evaluated for their success and the government only pays the funder (the bank) if the program meets the metrics. If the program exceeds the metrics, then the investor can receive bonus money, making the program much more expensive for the public and highly lucrative for the banks.

Banks love Pay for Success because they can profit massively from it and invest money with high returns at a time of a glut of capital and historically low interest rates. Politicians (especially rightist democrats) love Pay for Success because they can claim to be expanding public services without raising taxes or issuing bonds and will only have the public pay for "what works." Elite universities and corporate philanthropies love Pay for Success because they support "innovation" and share an ethos that only the prime beneficiaries of the current economy, the rich, can save the poor.

Pay for Success began as social impact bonds and were imported into the United States from the United Kingdom around 2010. They were promoted by the leading consultancy advocate of neoliberal education, McKinsey Consulting; the neoliberal think tank Center for American Progress, which was founded by former Clinton chief of staff and Democratic Party leader John Podesta (who also led Obama's transition); and the Rockefeller Foundation. Pay for Success expansion is now the central agenda of the Rockefeller Foundation. Shortly before championing Pay for Success for Chicago, Rahm Emanuel served as Obama's chief of staff, having had a long career as a hard-driving Democratic congressman and political money raiser and also an investment banker. Certain other key figures lobbied to expand the use of Pay for Success. Most notably, Jeffrey Liebman went from Obama's Office of Management and Budget to a large center at Harvard, the Government Performance Lab in the Kennedy School of Government, dedicated to expanding Pay for Success. Liebman is a leader of the Center for American Progress and was a key economic advisor to Obama in his 2008 campaign. Other key influencers of Pay for Success include the Rockefeller Foundation and Third Sector Capital.

Advocates explain that the value of a Pay for Success program is allegedly that it creates a "market incentive" for a bank or investor to fund a social program when there is not the *political will* to support the expansion of public services, and second, by injecting "market discipline" into the bureaucratically encumbered public sector, Pay for Success will make the public sector "*accountable*" through investment in "what works," and it will avoid funding public programs for which the public has "little to show," as Liebman and Third Sector Capital Partners are fond of suggesting (Wallace, 2014).[3] The value of any public spending in this view must be *measurable* through quantitative metrics to be of social value. Third, it consequently *saves money* by not funding programs that cannot be shown to be effective, and fourth, it *shifts risk* away from the public and onto the private sector while retaining only the potential social benefit for the public. Last, it mobilizes beneficent corporations, banks, powerful nonprofit companies, and philanthropic foundations to save the poor, the powerless, and the public from themselves. Here Goldman Sachs frames its profit-seeking activities as *corporate social responsibility*, charity, and good works that define its image in the public mind. In fact, all five of these positions that advocates claim explicitly or implicitly to support the expansion of Pay for Success are baseless.

3. Nicole Wallace, "With a Few Pay-for-Success Plans Under Way, the Idea Is Gaining Currency and Criticism," *Chronicle of Philanthropy* 26, no. 15 (2014): 1–23.

The Myths of Pay for Success

Myth 1: Market Discipline

Repeating a long-standing neoliberal mantra of private-sector efficiency and public-sector bloat, advocates of Pay for Success claim that the programs are necessary because they inject a healthy dose of *market discipline* into the bureaucratically encumbered and unaccountable public sphere. According to the leading proponent of Pay for Success, Jeffrey Liebman, private-sector finance produces this market discipline because governments do not monitor and measure the services contractors provide. Says Liebman, "[Government] programs that don't produce results continue to be financed year after year, something that would not happen in the business world."[4] This is an odd claim from one of Obama's leading economic advisors at the time that Obama was sworn in as president and who proceeded to have the public sector bail out the private sector. The 2008 financial bailout of the banks by the U.S. federal government represents a repudiation of the neoliberal logic of the natural discipline of markets and of deregulation. The private sector, including banks, insurance companies, and the automotive industry, needed the public sector to step in and save unprofitable businesses and businesses that had invested in the deregulated mortgage-backed securities market. More broadly, some of the largest sectors of the economy, such as defense, agriculture, and entertainment, rely on massive public-sector subsidies to function. Specifically, the financial crisis and consequent recession were a result first of neoliberal bank deregulation and a faith in markets to regulate themselves, but also they demonstrated the illegal activity, fraud, and lies of the same banks that now seek profit through Pay for Success, including Goldman Sachs, Bank of America, Merrill Lynch, and J. P. Morgan.

4. Martha Ann Overland, "Paying for Results: A New Approach to Government Aid," *Chronicle of Philanthropy* 23, no. 7 (2011): 9.

Pay for Success proponents claim that the financing scheme is necessary because there would otherwise not be the *political will* to do projects like early childhood education in Chicago for a couple of thousand children or recidivism reduction programs in Massachusetts. Third Sector Capital Partners, a nonprofit that relies on Pay for Success expansion as a cornerstone of its business, claims that Americans do not support state spending and hence Pay for Success is necessary.[5] However, Gallup shows that 75 percent of Americans favor expanded public spending on infrastructure, and 58 percent support replacing the Affordable Care Act with a universal federal health care system.[6] Indeed, as long-standing studies and, more recently, the Bernie Sanders presidential campaign of 2016 indicate, a large percentage of Americans support a range of increased spending on progressive social programs.

A mantra found in the literature that advocates Pay for Success is that it "allow[s] the government to avoid paying for programs that don't make a difference."[7] For working-class and poor citizens, many of whom are working two or three low-paying jobs, the cost of private early childcare and education is a major financial burden. The fact that early childcare and education have become corporatized by national companies who pay superexploitative wages to workers only worsens the situation. The fact that early childcare and education are vital economic needs raises a question about *whose political will* is in question when Pay for Success pro-

5. Drew Von Glahn and Caroline Whistler, "Pay for Success Programs: An Introduction," *Policy and Practice,* June 2011.

6. Frank Newport, "Americans Say Yes to Spending More on VA," Gallup, March 21, 2016, http://www.gallup.com/poll/190136/americans -say-yes-spending-infrastructure.aspx?g_source=federal%20spending& g_medium=search&g_campaign=tiles; Newport, "Majority in U.S. Support Fed-Funded Healthcare System," Gallup, May 16, 2016, http://www.gallup .com/poll/191504/majority-support-idea-fed-funded-healthcare-system .aspx?g_source=Politics&g_medium=newsfeed&g_campaign=tiles.

7. Overland, "Paying for Results."

ponents claim that the only way to provide early child educational services is with the involvement of banks, and that without banks, it should not be provided. The parents and community members are not the ones who lack the political will. Political and financial elites do not want to pay for other people's children—without a cut.

Myth 2: Transfer of Risk from the Public to the Private

The elaborate involvement of banks, lawyers, for-profits, and nonprofit coordinating companies appears more than superfluous when one takes a closer look at what is actually being done with Pay for Success in Chicago through the expansion of pre-K to twenty-six hundred Chicago public school children. Chicago mayor Rahm Emanuel's office lists six schools on the west and south sides and reports, "[Chicago Public Schools] and its teachers will manage the expanded program in these schools for the current academic year and expand to additional schools in future years."[8] If the program simply expands existing CPS programs with already employed teachers and administrators, then the potentially significantly higher cost of using Pay for Success makes little sense. In other words, why not just expand the existing successful services, such as the parent–child centers that have been successful in Chicago since 2002? According to the mayor's office, the risk is worth it because Pay for Success "is structured to insure that its lenders, the Goldman Sachs Social Impact Bond Fund and Northern Trust as senior lenders, and the J.B. and M.K. Pritzker Family Foundation as a subordinate lender, are only repaid if students realize positive academic results."[9] However, critics of Pay for Success point out that in reality, there is little risk

8. Mayor's Press Office, "Mayor Emanuel Announces Expansion of Pre-K to More than 2,600 Chicago Public School Children," City of Chicago, October 7, 2014, http://www.cityofchicago.org/city/en/depts/mayor/press _room/press_releases/2014/oct/mayor-emanuel-announces-expansion-of -pre-k-to-more-than-2-600-ch.html.

9. Mayor's Press Office.

for investors of losing that $17 million because the investors select already proven projects, such as those in Chicago.[10] Indeed, they are more likely to make the millions more in profit as in the $30 million that Goldman was paid back.[11] As Melissa Sanchez of the *Chicago Reporter* points out, investors not only make profits but additionally receive positive public relations, goodwill, and image boosting.[12] This is not a small matter for a bank such as Goldman Sachs, which was in the center of the subprime mortgage crisis and was found to have committed both illegal and unethical investment practices.

Risk is also mitigated for the banks by philanthropies, such as Rockefeller and Bloomberg, that guarantee repayment of the money the banks invest.[13] Even its proponents admit that Pay for Success is "not a panacea," as banks are not really willing to take risks and, consequently, are only willing to consider about 20 percent of service providers.[14] The attractive service providers are the ones with established track records that all but guarantee success. Pay for Success cannot be justified as an innovative scheme that transfers the risk taking of the market into the public sector while transferring financial risk out of the public sector and onto markets.

Economist David Macdonald points out the extent to which the promise of risk transfer is in fact a lie. Macdonald explains that Pay for Success is not experimental. He argues that a bank such as Goldman Sachs is never going to put up $5 million with a 50 percent risk of losing its money, and so it will invest only in proven projects. Moreover, even if Goldman were to take a risk and the metrics did not pan out in its favor,

10. Melissa Sanchez, "Child–Parent Centers Boast Strong Results for Kids, Investors," *Chicago Reporter,* May 16, 2016.

11. Sanchez, "Investors Earn Max Initial Payment."

12. Sanchez, "Child–Parent Centers Boast Strong Results."

13. Quinton, "How Goldman Sachs Can Help Save the Safety Net," 1.

14. Overland, "Paying for Results," 9.

there's no way the government will refuse to pay Goldman Sachs back the full $5 million. Why? Because if Goldman Sachs loses $5 million or any part of it, it's not going to come back next year, and neither are any of the other bankers and private investors.[15]

Yet, even with the risk to bank profits eliminated by highly selective program selection, underwriting by philanthropies, and the government's desire to keep the bank coming back, as the Chicago example highlights, even if the leveraged Chicago Public Schools go bankrupt as the Republican investment banker governor of Illinois Bruce Rauner seems intent to cause, banks such as Goldman Sachs are first in line as creditors as the pieces of the system are sold off.[16] So rather than a system that injects the risk taking of markets into the public sector, Pay for Success injects capital drainage into successful programs while assuring minimal risk only for the profiteers. As Macdonald writes, the *inversion* of risk represents a disturbing change in whom government serves:

> People pay their taxes (and expect corporations to do so as well) in part because they want the government to deliver good services to the people who need them. But social impact bonds direct tax dollars to bank profits instead of to people in need. This dramatically changes who is being served by the government: from those who need a helping hand to affluent investors who need no government help at all.[17]

Myth 3: Accountability

Proponents also claim that Pay for Success programs are more accountable than the public sector because, allegedly, programs are

15. David Macdonald, "Anti-Philanthropy: Social Impact Bond the Worst Way to Fund Social Programs," *CCPA Monitor,* February 2013, 37.

16. Ben Joravsky, "Rahm's Latest Wall Street Bond Deal Is a Bad Deal for the City," *The Chicago Reader,* February 11, 2016, http://www.chicagoreader.com/Bleader/archives/2016/02/11/rahms-latest-wall-street-bond-deal-is-a-bad-deal-for-the-city.

17. Macdonald, "Anti-Philanthropy," 37.

measured independently. As the principles of Third Sector Capital write, "outcomes need to be tangible and measurable, such as reduced recidivism rates and lower utilization of foster care placement. The analyses of fiscal savings need to be demonstrated in quantifiable numbers, such as a reduction in special education dollars, lower Medicare payouts and lower juvenile justice expenditures."[18]

Yet critics of Pay for Success have raised issues about who is making the decisions about measurement and how benchmarks have been decided.[19] A basic problem with this argument for accountability through measurable outcomes is that, in practice, as a juvenile justice caseworker involved in recidivism reduction in a Massachusetts Pay for Success project explained to me, the caseworker received constant phone calls from an investment bank encouraging the caseworker to have the metrics turn out in favor of the bank so that the bank would earn the maximum amount possible through the bond. Indeed, what I heard directly from a participant in Pay for Success was a general concern of Jon Pratt, head of the Minnesota Council of Nonprofits. Pratt stated, "You're definitely creating incentives that would be considered corruption pressures." Pratt's point is that by having allegedly independent measurement tied to the possibility of profit or loss, a not-so-independent incentive is created to game the outcomes or cheat.

Such "corruption pressures" in neoliberal education reform have had a high profile as high-stakes standardized testing threatened to defund school districts, schools, and classrooms if test scores did not rise. Administrators and teachers, deeply concerned that poor students would lose desperately needed resources, found that the ethical action would be to cheat rather than participate in sanctifying the denial of resources to those most in need. Similarly, when the largest for-profit educational management

18. Von Glahn and Whistler, "Pay for Success Programs."
19. Overland, "Paying for Results," 5.

company, Edison Schools (now Edison Learning), was expanding in the 1990s and 2000s, its increased growth depended on continually raising more investor capital. The for-profit education company could only acquire capital by showing prospective investors increasingly rising test scores.[20] As a consequence, numerous test scandals erupted, and massive institutional pressure was placed on administrators and teachers to show raised test scores no matter what.

Other critics raise practical concerns with Pay for Success, including concern that organizational capacity of a service provider can be temporarily built up by a contract but "not build the organizations' capacity to support that growth."[21] As well, critics point to how time consuming these agreements are to create.[22] Contracts are so convoluted and complicated that what normally would take a month to do takes two years, and with financial arrangements so complicated that a university professor in financial management "still needed help understanding the financing."[23]

As the commissioned evaluation report makes clear, not only had Chicago's Pay for Success early childhood project received positive evaluations since 2002 but early childhood education interventions such as the child–parent center model have been measured and found to have positive effects on future academic performance since 1967.[24] Unsurprisingly, that is, early childhood learning initiatives have been known to result in measurable improvements in student performance in subsequent academic years. These facts raise obvious questions in response to Pay for

20. Saltman, *Edison Schools*.

21. Wallace, "With a Few Pay-for-Success Plans," 4.

22. Wallace, 4.

23. Liz Farmer, "The Hidden Cost to 'Pay for Success,'" *Governing*, November 12, 2015, http://www.governing.com/topics/finance/gov-cost-pay-for-success-social-impact-bonds.html.

24. E. Gaylor, T. Kutaka, K. Ferguson, C. Williamson, X. Wei, and D. Spiker, *Evaluation of Kindergarten Readiness in Five Child–Parent Centers: Report for 2014–15* (Menlo Park, Calif.: SRI International 2016), 16.

Success advocates' claims that private bank financing is needed to ensure measurable accountability.

An additional problem with accountability being understood strictly through numerically quantifiable measurement is that the problems of positivist ideology are brought into areas of educational service that are not necessary ideally measurable in quantitative terms. Positivist ideology treats knowledge and truth as a collection of facts and radically devalues examination of the theoretical assumptions behind claims to truth.[25] Knowledge in this view disregards both the relationship between learning and the interpretive practices and perspectives of subjects and the relationship between learning and the broader social world. As Pay for Success projects receive that $400 billion to $1 trillion, they will be used for a wider array of educational services, including many areas of schooling in which learning is interpretive and involves judgment, criticism, and analysis. Not necessarily always quantifiable, the development of such interpretive capacities does not always appear immediately but progresses over time. The message from the leaders of Pay for Success in that the government spends billions of dollars on public services that are not measured and hence has "little to show for it."[26] Implicit here is an assumption that that which cannot be immediately measured quantifiably also cannot be justified as a public expense. This presumes that the kinds of subjects that are less quantifiably measured, such as the humanities or abstract sciences, are less valuable and that funding in the future ought only to follow that which can be quantified.

The denial of interests and values renders the measurement fetish of accountability pseudo-science or scientism. For example, Goldman Sachs, J. P. Morgan, and Bank of America have all been seeking profit in Pay for Success. Each bank has paid the U.S. Department of Justice multi-billion-dollar settlements for not

25. Giroux, *Theory and Resistance in Education.*
26. Wallace, "With a Few Pay-for-Success Plans," 2.

prosecuting them for lying about the risks of subprime mortgage investments and defrauding investors in the run-up to the 2008 subprime crisis and Great Recession.[27] In 2011, confessed financial fraudster Goldman Sachs sought 22 percent profit on its investment of $9.6 million in a Riker's Island Pay for Success project *teaching moral reasoning* to juvenile inmates.[28] The efficacy of the project was to be measured by reduced recidivism. Shortly after lying and breaking the law for profit, Goldman Sachs received a contract from New York City's billionaire mayor Michael Bloomberg. Bloomberg's own philanthropy backed the Goldman Sachs investment so that, should the metrics not pan out, the bank would not lose money. While this particular Pay for Success project did not achieve the metrics, the value of the metrics themselves as an arbiter of the value of the project is profoundly suspect in that they shut down some of the most crucial questions that need to be asked of such a project, such as, Why would a company responsible for tanking the economy through fraud be hired to teach moral reasoning to youth? Why are the youth incarcerated in the first place, and what class and race position do they come from? Why did none of the leaders of Goldman Sachs or the other banks who broke the law in the financial crisis spend a day in prison, and what class and race positions do they come from? What are the broader structural and systemic patterns and power relations that produce these different lived realities of legal accountability for some and no accountability for others, such as the ways that a racialized class hierarchy is reproduced through mass incarceration, the finance industry, and the educational system? Who is authorized to develop the metrics, what is their expertise, what are their interests, and how do they assess the rules they set in place? To whom are those legislating the accountability measurements accountable? The scientism of metrics obscures these kinds

27. Lucinda Shen, "Goldman Sachs Finally Admits It Defrauded Investors during the Financial Crisis," *Fortune,* April 11, 2016.

28. Quinton, "How Goldman Sachs Can Help Save the Safety Net," 1.

of questions. Accountability should be a part of educational projects, but not through restricted metrics that conceal the broader politics informing the project. Rather, accountability should be in a form in which knowledge is comprehended in relation to how subjectivity is formed through broader social forces and in ways in which learning can form the basis for collective action to expand egalitarian and just social relations.

Myth 4: Cost Savings

A central argument of Pay for Success proponents is that they save money by only funding successful programs. However, as the prior sections suggest, if in fact evaluation is not independent and only already successful programs are being selected, and governments have incentives to continue contracting, and there are "corruption pressures," then the alleged "market discipline" through competition cannot work. Yet there is additional evidence that Pay for Success adds costs rather than cutting them.

Pay for Success introduces large expenses to fund extensive legal services to handle those convoluted and complicated contracts that take years instead of months.[29] Additionally, third-party project managers and evaluators add costs to the services.[30] If the metrics pan out for the investors, then they can earn more than double the money that they put up for the service.[31] The intensely time-consuming and convoluted deals cost more money for administration, and this cuts into the spending on the service itself.[32] The Department of Legislative Services in Maryland studied social impact bonds for recidivism reduction programs and found no

---

29. Melissa Sanchez, "For the Record: Paying for Preschool with Social Impact Bonds," *Chicago Reporter,* November 3, 2014, https://www.chicagoreporter.com/record-paying-preschool-social-impact-bonds/.

30. Sanchez.

31. Sanchez, 2.

32. Wallace, "With a Few Pay-for-Success Plans."

savings.[33] For prisons or schools with fixed costs, such as physical sites, saving in per inmate or student costs is not significant because it does not reduce the fixed costs.[34]

On the west side of Chicago, one of the billionaire heirs to the Hyatt hotel fortune, J. B. Pritzger, whose investment firm worked with Goldman Sachs on the Chicago early childhood Pay for Success project, cut the ribbon at an early childhood center and stated that such projects must be good investments to be successful.[35] Pritzger's statement aligns with a trend that has intensified since the advent of venture philanthropy and that has reimagined philanthropy as being similar to business.[36] Venture philanthropies hijack public governance, install corporate models and managerialism for public services, and promote public-sector privatization by steering the use of public money toward the private sector.[37] Venture philanthropies generally give money, and the giving results in a tax break for the corporation or individual who gives to the nonprofit. However, most venture philanthropies do not actually seek to get the money back, let alone with profit. Social impact bonds (aka Pay for Success), according to David Macdonald, are not philanthropy; they are, rather, "anti-philanthropy."[38] They are profit-seeking activity masquerading as philanthropy. Some venture philanthropy has a similar effect, such as when Gates and Microsoft privatize public education by the initiatives of the Gates Foundation for privatization schemes, technology dependency, and so on. However, not even venture philanthropy is explicitly organized as a for-profit business. Pay for Success is similar to CZI, launched in 2015, in which the "philanthropy" is actually a LLC that financially invests in other projects. As Macdonald sug-

33. Wallace, 5.

34. Wallace, 5.

35. Wallace, 6.

36. Saltman, *The Gift of Education: Public Education and Venture Philanthropy* (New York: Palgrave Macmillan, 2010).

37. Saltman.

38. Macdonald, "Anti-Philanthropy," 1.

gests, why not cut out the "middleman"? That is, why not cut out the banks seeking profit and the third parties and lawyers facilitating the deals?

Finally, a cost problem with Pay for Success is that, as critics contend, with private-sector lenders involved, interest rates will tend to be higher than with public-sector bond issuance. House Appropriations Committee chair Representative Ross Hunter blocked a federal social impact bond bill. He said, "As a private investor, what kind of interest rate are you going to ask for? Eleven percent? Nine percent? By contrast, interest rates on revenue bonds can be as low as 4%. If early learning is a good idea, I can issue [government-backed revenue] bonds to pay for it."[39] In Chicago, Goldman Sachs could more than double its initial investment of $16.6 million as the metrics determine that Goldman receives the maximum amount from the city under the agreement.[40] This is a much higher total cost to the public to provide the service to twenty-six hundred children than what a bond issuance would be.

Myth 5: Corporate Social Responsibility

For banks, corporate foundations, and venture philanthropies to claim that Pay for Success represents the goodwill of these actors, they must represent public-sector pillage as public-sector support and care. However, they must also position these private accumulation projects as necessary, inevitable, and without alternative. This is why proponents repeat the private-sector language about the "hopelessly bureaucratic public sector" needing "market discipline," private-sector "cost savings," "accountability," "financial innovation," and "risk reduction," despite evidence and reason to the contrary. The private-sector project of Pay for Success is one that involves not merely the private capture of public wealth but

39. J. Hoback, "Private Money, Public Impact," *State Legislatures,* May 2015, 26–29.

40. Sanchez, "Investors Earn Max Initial Payment."

also the public reframing of symbolic meanings that make such wealth capture possible, remaking common sense in ways that suggest that only the rich can promote just social change by pursuing their financial interests. Such ideologies suggest that the very private forces responsible for draining and weakening the public are in fact saviors for the public, that there is no alternative to markets in every social realm, that public citizens are nothing more than economic actors, and that these projects are apolitical rather than representing the interests and perspectives of capitalists over workers and most citizens. Nonprofits like the Center for American Progress, the Rockefeller Foundation, and Harvard are among the loudest boosters of Pay for Success. The ideological work that these organizations do shapes public perceptions about the morality and public impact of private-sector organizations like Goldman Sachs. In this sense, Pay for Success is a form of public relations for banks that the banks largely do not have to pay for. In fact, Pay for Success facilitates banks being paid by the public to promote this public relations bonanza. As with venture philanthropies, the public ends up not only financially subsidizing private banks but also subsidizing the loss of public control over public governance for public services. With venture philanthropies, the subsidy takes public revenues in the form of tax breaks for rich donors and corporations. With Pay for Success, the public pays a premium for services that could have been provided directly through the government and loses democratic governance control over the service.

Pay for Success/social impact bonds appeal to banks for their capacity to generate profits from public tax money for education, juvenile justice, and other services, and they represent a form of economic redistribution from desperately needed public money for the most vulnerable citizens, such as poor youth, to business. They also appeal to banks that got caught defrauding investors and that can now promote themselves as doing good works while turning a profit. Pay for Success also appeals to neoliberal politicians, such as Mayor Rahm Emanuel in Chicago, who can claim that they are doing "innovative finance" in the interest of taxpayers instead of raising taxes or issuing educational bonds. The reality is that politicians like Emanuel are just kicking the can down the road, as Pay for Success does not solve the historical failure to adequately fund public education or other social services (like the mental health services he gutted), just adding to the long-standing debt burden. In fact, because it costs more, social impact investing raises this debt burden, thereby destabilizing the public system further. In this sense, Pay for Success is an elaborate form of public relations that makes failing to address a public problem look like innovative action.

Pay for Success/social impact bonds ought to be understood simply as one of the latest efforts of the private sector to exploit and pillage the public sector for profit at a historical moment of uncertain economic growth and a crisis of capital accumulation. New legislation and policy must be developed to limit the access of investment banks to determining, running, and profiting from social programs.

Student Income Loans: Transferring Wealth to Investors, Risk to Students

AT MORE THAN $1.3 trillion as of 2016,[1] U.S. student loan debt has become widely discussed in the media, the business press, and academia as a new debt bubble with the potential to burst and trigger a global economic crisis that will put everyone at risk. The student debt bubble is regularly compared to the subprime mortgage debt bubble that resulted in the failure of banks, the Great Recession, and the public bailout of Wall Street and the auto industry in 2008. Prior to the subprime crisis, high- and low-risk mortgages were packaged together into investment bonds so that when enough of the high-risk mortgages defaulted, the bonds that had been rated as safe collapsed. Similarly, one form of student debt investment security, student loan asset-backed securities (SLABS), comprises pooled student debt.

A crucial difference between the subprime debt bubble and the student debt bubble is that the properties that comprised subprime mortgage securities served as collateral to the mortgage debt. If a homeowner defaults on a mortgage, the bank claims the property in its stead. Student loan debt has traditionally not been collateralized. In other words, if a student or former student defaults on student loans, there is no tangible asset for the bank to claim. However, since a great deal of student loan debt has been federally subsidized and especially reinsured, private banks that

---

1. https://www.businessinsider.com/student-loan-debt-state-of-the-union-2016-1.

package student loan debt into investment securities have been able to sell these investment securities because they carry the full faith and credit of the federal government. Despite having no collateral, they have the federal guarantee.

In 2010, the federal government ended the Federal Family Education Loan Program (FFELP) that federally subsidized and reinsured the private loans that formed the basis of most SLABS, opting to shift federally subsidized loans into direct federal loans issued through the Department of Education. Despite the end of FFELP, privately held student loan debt and securities based on it accumulated prior to 2010 remain a massive outstanding debt that is predominately serviced, managed, and collected by a single for-profit corporation, Navient, that spun off from Sallie Mae. Sallie Mae was a public bank that lent to students and was privatized by the Clinton administration. Navient faces criminal charges of illegal collection practices and defrauding borrowers and has come under fire,[2] most notably by Senator Elizabeth Warren. With federal insurance and subsidies removed on these privately held FFELP loans as of 2010, Wall Street lost its enthusiasm for securitizing newly issued unsecured private debt, despite the fact that bankruptcy laws make student loan debt extremely difficult to discharge through bankruptcy. Enter the student income loan.

After the end of FFELP in 2010, private investors developed student income loans (also known as income share agreements, or ISAs), an "innovative" financing technique to expand private student loans and develop a new kind of student debt investment security. Several for-profit and nonprofit companies, such as 13th Avenue Funding, Lumni, and Pave, created student income loans that provide tuition in exchange for a percentage of future income. These lenders pool the student income loans into invest-

2. Nika Knight, "Sen. Elizabeth Warren Calls for Total Overhaul of Student Loan System," *Common Dreams,* March 31, 2016.

ment securities. The financiers have presented student income loans as a service to students, providing another avenue of educational finance, and as an innovation in lending. Since the federal government does not insure or subsidize the loans, the private investors make terms that mitigate their risk while maximizing their profit. Profits can be enormous. The *Wall Street Journal* offers an example of a student ultimately paying $60,000 for a $15,000 tuition loan.[3]

One key way these student income loan banks limit risk and maximize profit is by restricting loan issuance to students who study subjects that are expected to result in high incomes, such as engineering, or by restricting loans to graduate students in select fields. This instrumental and vocational tendency of student income loans contributes to the rising clamor to defund elements of higher education that do not directly result in commercial benefits for business, such as programs in the humanities and the arts, the social sciences, and even the abstract sciences.

Other new, nontraditional private lenders[4] post-FFELP cater to what *Forbes* calls "the indebted 1%" because they have "racked up pricey and prestigious debt."[5] These banks capture the lowest-risk student borrowers from the outstanding pool of the student loan debt that is eligible for refinancing—75 percent of the $1.2 trillion in debt. Companies like CommonBond ($100 million refinanced) and SoFi ($1 billion refinanced) refinance student loan debt at lower rates than the federal government by cherry-picking the students and graduates who are seen as being at lowest risk of defaulting on their loans. By creaming off the highest-quality, that is, the lowest-risk, loans, SoFi and CommonBond are able to offer lower interest rates only to the

3. Douglas Belkin, "More College Students Selling Stock—in Themselves," *Wall Street Journal,* August 5, 2015, 5.

4. Maggie McGrath, "Student Debt as an Asset Class: A $1 Trillion Opportunity?," *Forbes,* December 10, 2014, 2.

5. McGrath.

minority of borrowers who have an average income of more than $130,000 yet raise the overall risk of other pooled federal student debt.

Another way student income loans limit risk for investors is by banks pooling loans together in tranches (like subprimes). Some student income loan arrangements pool debtors together and make the default by one debtor to cause the interest rates (percentage of future income taken) for all borrowers to rise. Lenders like to make these pools of debtors out of students from the same alma mater so that there is an additional sense of affiliation and moral obligation to fellow students. This arrangement adds a moral culpability onto the borrower in such a way as to counter the rationality of *homo economicus* that drives these projects. Why, after all, wouldn't a rational economic actor seek to default on these loans in which the only collateral is their future work and goodwill? By linking the fate of other borrowers in the investment security, lenders levy on debtors a social stake in not defaulting (you, borrower, are screwing not just the rich, greedy banker but also your fellow student, who has a precarious situation like yours). Of course, the truly social act would be to dispense with the debt altogether and make the social obligation one for the entire society rather than restricted communities of borrowers to bear.

Student income loans and other new, nontraditional private student loans represent not merely a new form of student loan financing but also (1) a form of *upward economic redistribution* in the context of a broader assault on public institutions, particularly on public higher education, and a downward transfer of responsibility and risk onto youth; (2) a force for the neoliberal *vocationalization and instrumentalism* of higher education that participates in the broader trend driven by neoliberal privatization and corporate culture; and (3) a form of *indenture* that relies on the fabrication of a specific form of restricted morality and the capture of future forms of associated living. I suggest that these three key elements of student income loans need to be seen as a material and symbolic project of class warfare waged by the rich on the rest.

Following the Great Recession of 2008 and the ensuing rightist push for austerity, states and the federal government significantly cut public higher education spending. Universities responded by raising tuition. As is common during recessions, university enrollments increased. As students assumed debt to pay for university, an effective redistributive transfer was accomplished whereby youth, among the most economically vulnerable citizens, absorbed the costs. A number of states not only cut higher education funding but also enacted educational privatizations and created slush funds for businesses. While spending has not been fully restored, students are shouldering the debt burden, and banks are profiting.

Higher education spending cuts by states need to be seen as effectively an upward redistribution scheme, with tuition increasing by the same amount as public defunding: about 10 percent. Thirty-six percent of undergraduates take federal student loans, and 6 percent take more expensive private loans. Forty-seven percent of public higher education revenue comes from tuition. The state defunding of public higher education is regressive, much like the shift from an income tax to a sales tax, in that it puts more of the burden on a smaller segment of the population while lifting the burden to pay for this public good through taxation off of those with greater wealth and income.

The federal government also cut education spending in the wake of the recession. To make matters worse, the federal government "generated upwards of $100 billion in revenues from its student loan operations from 2008 to 2013."[6] To put this federal revenue generation in context, the money that students pay to the federal government joins a pool of money that in the age of austerity decreasingly goes to pay for the caregiving functions of the federal government but increasingly goes to pay for its punitive functions. Perhaps most perniciously, half of federal discretionary

---

6. Jack Du, "Student Loan Asset-Backed Securities: Safe or Subprime?," Investopedia, http://www.investopedia.com/articles/investing /081815/student-loan-assetbacked-securities-safe-or-subprime.asp.

spending goes toward the military and military-related spending, while enormous amounts go to subsidize private industries, such as corporate agriculture and entertainment. In this regard, the shift of the costs of higher education onto students represents a kind of debt spending by youth to fund the military and corporations. This generational pillage is not just unethical; it represents an economic burden on future workers and consumers who will be spending to service debt to create bank profits. In addition to being a financial redistribution, it is also a *transfer of risk and responsibility.*

As Andrew Ross explains, the transfer of fiscal responsibility from the state to the individual is a key aspect of higher education privatization.[7] He points out that it would only cost $87 billion to federally fund every two- and four-year public college. This is a miniscule amount relative to the $1.22 trillion spent annually by the federal government on tax breaks and less than the current $102 billion federal outlay for education that represents just 2.67 percent of all federal spending.

Student income loans further the vocationalizing and instrumentalizing trend that has been expanding with the corporatization of higher education. The AEI, an outspoken neoliberal advocate of student income loans, or ISAs, writes,

> Because ISA investors earn a profit only when a student is successful, they offer students better terms for programs that are expected to be of high value and have strong incentives to support students both during school and after graduation. This process gives students strong signals about which programs and fields are most likely to help them be successful.[8]

In this context, "successful" means students endeavoring to pursue the highest-paying fields that are the most directly commer-

7. Andrew Ross, "Mortgaging the Future: Student Debt in the Age of Austerity," *New Labor Forum* 22, no. 1 (2013): 23–28.

8. As quoted in Jeff Bryant, "Wall Street's New Student Loan Scheme: Subprime Loans Are Coming to Financial Aid," *Salon,* March 30, 2015, 8.

cializable. As Jeff Bryant of *Salon* writes, this will likely lead to students being pushed into academic programs that are "financially incentivized" by investors rather than toward programs that appeal to students' imaginations, ideas, or interests.

Bryant suggests that the danger of the vocational tendencies of student income loans lies not only in restricting the pursuit of meaningful, passionate, and interesting work but also in its harm to business, because "outliers" from the humanities often make important contributions to business. He emphasizes that unless the interests and desires of a young student are math or science, "a quest for personal development and intrinsic reward . . . becomes a lifelong liability regardless of personal attributes."

Moreover, making majors in the humanities, arts, and social sciences more expensive will result in the further gutting of these programs from universities and a reduction in the number of not only workers but also citizens who are educated in the knowledge and habits of society and self-reflection grounded in traditions of culture and scholarly thought. There is more at stake than just individual economic opportunity. As Henry Giroux argues, the undermining of the humanities as part of the war on public higher education represents the production of civic illiteracy in that it deprives citizens of the intellectual tools to interpret and intervene in public problems and fosters "organized forgetting" as history is flattened into a permanent present understood through private acts of working and consuming.[9]

These public and civic concerns expressed by Giroux seem not to be on the minds of the financiers behind student income loans. McGrath writes,

> "Not to be glib about it," says Tom Glocer, former Thomson Reuters CEO and a CommonBond equity investor, "but if you're coming to me for a loan and you're a dentistry student at the University of

9. Henry Giroux, "Authoritarian Politics in the Age of Civic Illiteracy," Counterpunch, April 15, 2016, https://www.counterpunch.org/2016/04/15/authoritarian-politics-in-the-age-of-civic-illiteracy/.

Pennsylvania, I'll be more willing to make a loan than if you tell me you're an art history major at Texas Christian."[10]

Student income loans do not only allow the rich to own the labor of another; they also allow the rich to create investment securities out of these collected pledges of future time and work while supporting the institutions that have historically bolstered their own class interests. These speculative instruments then serve as the basis for additional future private lending and, in turn, yet more speculation. Ultimately, student income loans not only promote a strictly commercial way of seeing education and its social value and defund fields of study alleged to have little commercial value; they also create a financial incentive to avoid mass public funding of higher education while fueling a dangerous educational debt bubble.

Rather than curtailing the subpriming of student debt by eliminating student income loans and seeking to reduce the student debt bubble, Trump's secretary of education, Betsy Devos, has aggressively sought to deregulate student lending for the benefit of banks and for-profit universities. Once in office, Devos appointed leaders from the for-profit higher education sector whose schools were being investigated for fraud. For-profit colleges and universities have engaged in widespread lying to prospective students about the value of a degree and the nature of a program to capture vast sums through tuition financed through student loan debt. Devos and these officials proceeded to dismantle the special team responsible for fraud investigations, and they also moved to protect colleges and universities that made fraudulent claims to students by gutting the "borrower's defense" act. Such flagrant disregard for fact, truth, and evidence is part of a pattern of gangster capitalism in which financial accumulation in higher education is based on fraudulent promises of future wealth for students and misrepresentation of the programs. This is exemplified by Trump

10. McGrath, "Student Debt as an Asset Class."

University, which closed after a pattern of defrauding students who were encouraged to go into massive debt on the pretext that they would become rich after taking real estate training. Following lawsuits, Trump settled, paying out $25 million.

The solution to the student debt crisis is not Obama-style regulation that makes universities justify their financial value to students based on earnings after graduation. The solution is a public investment in broad-based student debt forgiveness and universal free university education. These moves would not only eliminate the specter of a $1.3 trillion lending default that could tank the economy; they would also produce a massive economic stimulus that would benefit the bulk of the population rather than benefiting primarily the superrich and corporations while worsening the national debt as republican tax reform does.

"Philanthrocapitalism" and Personalized Learning: The Case of the Chan Zuckerberg Initiative

IN 2017, Mark Zuckerberg gave the commencement address at Harvard University, his alma mater, which he famously quit in his sophomore year to create Facebook. Zuckerberg, the fifth richest person in the world, had previously contributed $100 million to corporate school reform in Newark, New Jersey, in a project launched in 2010 that particularly focused on replacing public schools with privately managed charters and weakening teaching as a secure profession.[1] Zuckerberg's privatization initiative in Newark was marked by its antipathy to democratic and community control over schools in a district suffering from historical disinvestment and the related ills of racialized class inequality.[2] As Dale Russakoff details in *The Prize,* the restructuring of the Newark schools began with sham community information-gathering meetings that presented the public with a false sense of involvement. Secretly, Mark Zuckerberg, Newark mayor Cory Booker, and Governor Chris Christie had already planned the corporate school reform fate of Newark's public schools.[3] Zuckerberg was deeply involved with key figures and organizations across the political spectrum dedicated to the radical business-led transformation of public schools by privatizing ownership and control over

1. Dale Russakoff, *The Prize: Who's in Charge of America's Schools* (New York: Mariner Books, 2016).
2. Russakoff.
3. Russakoff.

schools, administration, teaching, and curriculum.[4] Privatization in this context referred to redistributing control from the community, teachers, and teacher's unions to superrich individuals and politicians.

In his Harvard address in 2017, Zuckerberg discussed his second major foray into education, CZI, emphasizing how his "for-profit philanthropy" focused on online personalized learning that would create meaningfulness and purpose for students by providing them the "freedom to fail" as they become entrepreneurs. Zuckerberg acknowledged that his own financial successes were only possible due to the economic privilege he inherited that provided him financial support and security to take entrepreneurial risk. Zuckerberg spoke of a new social contract with a universal basic income and lifelong educational services to confront the coming joblessness and insecurity brought about by technological innovation, of which, he neglected to mention, he has been both contributor and beneficiary. Zuckerberg recognized in his speech the extent to which economic success of individuals depends on support and security, and he advocated expanding the safety net in the interest of fostering a culture of business entrepreneurship. Zuckerberg's apparently liberal commitments to expanding the safety net are toward the end of a neoliberal vision of inclusion defined by markets and entrepreneurialism. Everyone should be supported to "fail up" aided by continuous education. And Zuckerberg's companies, Facebook and CZI, will be there to supply the lifelong learning products. Yet Zuckerberg did not mention in his address that CZI, LLC was a for-profit education company. Instead, he described it as a charity.

Zuckerberg and his wife, Priscilla Chan, had announced CZI on Facebook upon the birth of their daughter in 2015. At that time, they claimed that they were fulfilling Bill Gates's "giving pledge,"

4. See Russakoff. Some of the key organizations included Democrats for Education Reform, McKinsey Consulting, and New Schools Venture Fund, among many others.

which challenged billionaires to commit to give away the bulk of their fortunes. Zuckerberg and Chan alleged that they were pledging 99 percent of their Facebook stock, or $45 billion, to the new philanthropy. Yet, Zuckerberg and Chan gave their gift not to a philanthropic foundation but rather to their own LLC—an organization that shared staff, leadership, and a profit motive with Facebook. Whereas Facebook is a publicly traded corporation, CZI is privately held.

CZI follows the lead of Steve Jobs's billionaire widow Laurene Powell Jobs's for-profit LLC Emerson Collective and billionaire PayPal cofounder Pierre Omidyar's Omidyar Network.[5] All three of these companies target public schools for profit and participate in the neoliberal restructuring of public education while framing their profit-seeking, union-busting, standardization-promoting, and anticritical activities as "philanthropy"—a gift to children, schools, and the public.[6] All three promote themselves as "innovative" for selling technology products to public schools.

CZI in several ways expresses a view of education that affirms the concentration of economic, cultural, and political power; it promotes a pedagogical format that appears to emphasize individual student control while undermining education as dialogic and democratic and shifting control over curriculum and pedagogy away from teachers and communities and toward for-profit corporations. CZI also functions as effective public relations for Zuckerberg and Facebook as they have come under fire for disseminating fake news during the 2016 presidential election and for live streaming murders and suicides.[7] The first section discusses CZI's redefinition of philanthropy and the importance of

5. Omidyar Network has both a for-profit LLC and a nonprofit wing.

6. Omidyar Network invests in numerous for-profit education companies, including for-profit Bridge International Academies, which has faced extensive criticism around the world for its actions, performance, and school model. CZI also invests in Bridge International Academies.

7. Mike Isaac, "On the Road, Out of His Bubble," *New York Times,* May 26, 2017, B1.

recognizing CZI primarily as a for-profit business. The second section discusses CZI's "personalized learning" projects and how they displace teachers and the possibilities of democratic educational practices while creating the conditions for profit.

Misrepresenting Profit as Philanthropy

CZI has been widely discussed in the popular press for the controversial LLC form. Most accounts discuss the advantage to billionaires of retaining the greatest degree of control over the use of their money. The for-profit approach to "philanthropy" has been termed by some as *philanthrocapitalism*. However, there is vast confusion in the popular press and academia as to whether the term refers to the application of business ideals, corporate culture, and a private-sector approach to charity (as typified by nonprofit venture philanthropy foundations, such as Gates, Walton, and Broad) or to the declaration of a for-profit company itself as a philanthropy (CZI, Emerson, Omidyar). For-profit corporations cannot meaningfully be considered philanthropy.

Unlike nonprofit philanthropic foundations, which must release tax reports on the use of money, LLCs can do absolutely anything with the money in them without disclosing what they do.[8] Money in the LLC could be taken as profit, invested in educational projects, or moved to other for-profit businesses, such as Facebook, or arms dealing for that matter, and there is no way for the public to know. Money can be withdrawn freely, and unlike with nonprofits, there is no requirement that a portion of funds be used for the mission. Indeed, CZI could do nothing at all, and nobody would be the wiser.[9] Furthermore, unlike tax-exempt nonprofit foundations, for-profit LLCs can conduct political lobbying and can do so

8. Jocalyn Clark and Linsey McGoey, "The Black Box Warning on Philanthrocapitalism," *The Lancet* 388 (2016): 2457–59.

9. Daniel Dykes and Michael S. Schwartz, "The Chan Zuckerberg Initiative," *Trusts and Estates,* May 2016.

secretly.[10] CZI and other LLCs do not shelter income from taxes, but they can write off business losses and get tax benefits that way.

As I detailed in my book *The Gift of Education: Public Education and Venture Philanthropy,* the early 1990s began a shift from traditional or "scientific philanthropy" typified by Carnegie and Rockefeller to "venture philanthropy."[11] Scientific philanthropy, which held sway in the twentieth century, was animated by industrial capitalists' desire to support and expand the public sphere in part to bolster a meritocratic ideology. Public knowledge sources, such as libraries, museums, and schools, would allow individual citizens the means to acquire knowledge for private-sector development and public participation. Moreover, Carnegie was deeply worried about the growth of radical social movements, especially communism, and saw philanthropy as a means of undermining them by funding public institutions in ways compatible with the maintenance of elite economic and political rule.[12] Traditional philanthropists simultaneously supported the expansion of public institutions and promoted the redistributed burden for social opportunity onto individuals who had better be willing to work hard to acquire knowledge and culture to compete for social ascendance. Giving, for scientific philanthropy, was largely publicly oriented and largely granted control over the uses of the money to the recipient public institutions.

In contrast, venture philanthropy (VP), which began in Silicon Valley in the early 1990s, promotes a financial agenda of public-sector privatization and deregulation while remaking philanthropy on the model of corporate culture. The language of VP is derived from tech start-ups and venture capital. For VP,

10. Martin Levine, "Chan Zuckerberg LLC: No Tax Breaks + No Accountability = What Exactly?" *Non-Profit Quarterly,* December 7, 2015.

11. Saltman, *Gift of Education.*

12. See Andrew Carnegie, *The Gospel of Wealth,* 1889, https://www .carnegie.org/publications/the-gospel-of-wealth/. See also the important scholarship of Joan Roelofs and Robert Arnove on the uses of philanthropy for elite rule.

charity is positioned as an "investment" with outcomes termed "return on investment." Money is to be "leveraged" and initiatives to be "scaled up." Venture philanthropists endow their own nonprofit foundations, and get tax breaks to do so, but then largely retain control over the uses of the money. Most significantly, these uses involve privatizing public goods and services, such as schools, and promoting the ideology of corporate culture. For example, of the big three venture philanthropies, the Gates Foundation most aggressively promoted charter expansion, the Walton Foundation promoted vouchers, and the Broad Foundation promoted deregulating and privatizing educational leadership on the model of the corporation and database tracking projects. Venture philanthropists leverage their funds by often staging competitions among states, districts, and schools for scarce money. VP has created what I term elsewhere a "new market bureaucracy," in which the public bureaucracy has been denigrated as hopelessly inefficient and yet new layers of privately controlled organizations, such as charter funding and lobbying organizations, have been rolled out at the local, state, and national levels.[13]

VP-style "leveraging" as a model of influence was adopted by the Obama administration's signature Race to the Top program. It dangled money in front of states in exchange for aggressive efforts at expanding test-based accountability and lifting caps on charter expansion. There is an unvirtuous circle in which corporations and the superrich lobby to maintain low taxes that result in the inadequate funding of public infrastructure, and they lobby to get specific educational policies legislated that promote private-sector responses.[14] Then venture philanthropists get tax

13. Saltman, *Failure of Corporate School Reform.*
14. The big four educational publishers invested millions in lobbying for test-based accountability and made billions of dollars of profit as a consequence. Valerie Strauss, "Big Education Firms Spend Millions Lobbying for Pro-Testing Policies," *Washington Post,* March 30, 2015. See Kenneth

benefits to put their money into foundations that they control to influence and shape the public sphere—often in ways that allow them to pillage and profiteer, such as getting for-profits into the public sector. Venture philanthropies have managed to strategically influence the use of public money toward privatization and corporatization projects while allowing the billionaire donors to have outsized influence over these initiatives. For example, two of the largest recent educational reform pushes, charter schooling and the Common Core State Standards, were so massively promoted by the Gates Foundation that it is unlikely that they would have been implemented nearly at the scale they have without it. In this sense, venture philanthropists have managed to hijack governance from the public with regard to the use and direction of public wealth and decision-making.

VP ought to be understood as profoundly political in that it reallocates political control over public institutions and influences the priorities of them. As well, it transforms social relationships and culture in institutions in vertical and authoritarian as opposed to democratic ways, largely by promoting the ideologies of corporate culture. For example, public schooling has the potential to create the conditions for democracy by providing the knowledge and dispositions for collective democratic self-governance. Yet the accountability and charter movements aggressively promoted by venture philanthropists promoted rigid and repressive pedagogical approaches while shifting curriculum decisions to private control. VP has played a central

---

J. Saltman, "Corporate Schooling Meets Corporate Media: Standards, Testing, and Technophilia," *Review of Education Pedagogy Cultural Studies* 38, no. 2 (2016): 105–23. On the topic of lobbying and influence peddling by education corporations, see Helen Gunter and Colin Mills, *Consultants and Consultancy: The Case of Education* (Cham, Switzerland: Springer, 2017); Helen Gunter, David Hall, and Michael Apple, *Corporate Elites and the Reform of Public Education* (Bristol, U.K.: Policy Press, 2017), and Wayne Au and Jospeh Ferrara, *Mapping Corporate Education Reform: Politics and Power in the Neoliberal State* (New York: Routledge, 2016).

role in delinking public schooling from its formative capacities in democratic society, fostering instead a conception of schooling for private training for work and consumption.

While VP has de-democratizing tendencies in part by privatizing ownership and control over the public sphere, it is nonetheless philanthropy. In contrast, philanthrocapitalism, as typified by CZI, Emerson, and Omidyar, is mistakenly discussed in both mass media and academia as philanthropy albeit with greater secrecy and less transparency because it does not have to file tax forms disclosing its activities. Philanthrocapitalism in the form of the LLC should not be considered philanthropy but rather business. Writing in the *New York Times,* Singer and Isaac announced CZI with the headline "Mark Zuckerberg's Philanthropy Uses L.L.C. for More Control."[15] They went on to explain the advantages to the LLC form for Zuckerberg, including for-profit investment, political activity, fewer rules, and no disclosure. They conclude, "In all those ways, the L.L.C. acts more like a private investment vehicle for the couple."[16] While they are right that CZI acts like a private investment vehicle, it is impossible for anyone ever to find out what CZI really does in terms of giving or business. It is a mistake to describe CZI as philanthropy. The British medical journal *The Lancet* warns, "When it comes to the Chan Zuckerberg Initiative, the public may never know—and we have no legal right to know—whether any of the promised charity will actually go to charity at all."[17] Similarly, attorneys Dykes and Schwartz, writing in the journal *Trusts and Estates,* point out that "the donor has near total flexibility to change the LLC's mission or projects at any time and has wide latitude to engage in self-dealing. . . . And because the

15. Natasha Singer and Mike Isaac, "Mark Zuckerberg's Philanthropy Uses L.L.C. for More Control," *New York Times,* December 2, 2015.

16. Singer and Isaac.

17. Clark and McGoey, "Black Box Warning on Philanthrocapitalism," 2458.

promise to contribute to the LLC is unenforceable, the founder needn't even follow through on the plan of funding the LLC at all and can unfund it at any time."[18]

CZI's secrecy and privacy need to be seen in the context of the earlier Zuckerberg corporate school reform activities in Newark. Zuckerberg sought to reform schools while circumventing public participation in policy enactment. He was criticized for actively excluding the public from planning. Furthermore, the reforms themselves, such as the chartering, faced public criticism. The LLC form appears to be intended to specifically circumvent public accountability. However, there is a serious question as to whether CZI functions philanthropically at all or whether its activities are only profit seeking and "philanthropy" is a label intended to project an image of "corporate social responsibility."

VP already significantly redefined charitable giving by eroding the distinction between private good and public good. Nonprofit foundations like Gates, Walton, and Broad promote the idea that public problems are ideally addressed through private-sector solutions, that only the rich can save the poor, that the private sector is always more efficient and less bureaucratically encumbered than the public sector, and that public institutions, such as public schools, ought to be privatized and corporatized for their own good.

Perhaps most insidiously, VP contributes to a neoliberal reimagining of obligation in which private individuals are only responsible to themselves but not to the other members of the public. The LLC corporate form of CZI continues yet goes beyond VP's efforts to celebrate private dominance over public goods and services. Philanthrocapitalism represents an effort to collapse the distinction between public and private spheres and between profit seeking and charity. For example, a number of writers assume that for-profit "philanthropies" need to show both financial returns

18. Dykes and Schwartz, "Chan Zuckerberg Initiative."

and "social returns."[19] Because LLCs are not required to reveal their finances or activities, the distinction between these activities could not be ascertained. Nonetheless, giving the LLC the benefit of the doubt, these imperatives for financial and social returns are often in conflict, as they are with any business corporation, and the pursuit of profit comes at the expense of social returns, that is, the public interest when the survival of the business is at stake.[20] Zuckerberg largely profits through providing free content generated by other users and selling advertising on that volunteered content, while most philanthropy supports nonprofit causes that are intended to serve the public interest. These contradictory aims of wealth extraction and public purpose become glaringly obvious with CZI's central project of personalized learning and data extraction and its aims of replacing teacher labor with automated programs.

CZI's "Personalized Learning" Projects

Pay-for-Fee Services

Some of CZI's for-profit educational investments follow a profit model of pay-for-fee services. CZI invested $50 million in the BYJU's (Think and Learn Pvt. Ltd.) for-profit educational app that teaches mostly math, science, and test preparation, with its largest audience in India. Parents pay for the courses and subscription. This represents a development of neoliberal education that the World Bank has been promoting for years—pay-for-fee privatized education instead of the development of free universal public education in developing countries.[21] It deepens the ed-

19. Levine, "Chan Zuckerberg LLC."
20. For a valuable discussion of the incompatibility of corporate social responsibility and the corporation, see Joel Bakan, *The Corporation* (New York: The Free Press, 2005).
21. See James Tooley, *The Beautiful Tree* (Washington, D.C.: Cato, 2009).

ucational privatization that Chubb, Moe, and other U.S. rightists have been advocating through the use of technology,[22] namely, "unbundling" the school and treating each piece of what a school does as a commercializable service.

CZI is investing in for-profit educational technology companies like BYJU's, whose primary goal is the accumulation of wealth by selling to end users and public school districts and cutting costs to maximize profit. The profit motive results in an effort to extract money from the educational process by maximizing the amount of money taken in by the company and minimizing business expenses for labor, materials, and other overhead. BYJU's appears poised to compete globally for educational spending, as following the CZI investment, it purchased Edurite and Tutorvista from educational for-profit giant Pearson. The big take in these purchases was not so much these companies as their databases of students, including millions of U.S. students.[23] The acquisition of student data is at the center of personalized learning as a business.

Personalized learning itself developed out of commercial marketing applications. As an announcement of CZI's $50 million investment in for-profit education company BYJU's puts it, "personalization is a theme long pursued by consumer internet companies, especially e-trailers, who offer consumers a bouquet of choices to pick from based on their past shopping or browsing history. This in turn increases a consumer's engagement on the platform and significantly increases probability of a purchase."[24] While there is

22. See Terry M. Moe and John E. Chubb, *Liberating Learning* (San Francisco: Jossey-Bass, 2009). This kind of advocacy for debundling and privatizing through technology can be found in the advocacy of right-wing think tanks like Hoover and AEI.

23. Sindhu Kashyap, "Why BYJU's Chose to Bet on Edurite and Tutorvista," *Your Story,* May 15, 2017, https://yourstory.com/2017/05/byjus -edurite-tutorvista/.

24. Sayan Chakraborty, "BYJU's Updates App, Aims to Make Profits This Year," *LiveMint,* May 24, 2017, https://www.livemint.com/Companies /W0pmP4tPipqmo8ozq9lMDJ/Byjus-updates-app-aims-to-make-profits -this-year.html.

no widely agreed upon definition of personalized learning, proponents allege curriculum and pedagogy to be relevant to and tailored to students' interests. However, personalized learning has come to be associated with educational technology products that are designed to standardize and "deliver" content regardless of the specificities of the student, the teacher, or the context.

Summit and the Trade in Student Data

CZI bought Summit Charter School Network and has been promoting the implementation of Summit personalized learning technology in public schools around the United States. Summit is connected to advertising-driven Facebook, using software engineers to develop its online education platform. While Summit is initially given to schools without a fee, like Facebook, it collects user data. The connection to Facebook raises troubling school commercialism implications regarding the imposition of advertising in the classroom, the uses of private data, and the nonconsensual gathering of private, personal information from minors.

Unlike its investment in BYJU's, CZI's personalized learning project Summit does not profit by providing a fee for service. Summit enters use agreements directly with schools and hence becomes a part of the required curriculum. Facebook profits in part through advertising and in part by selling user data. While the pilot Summit Basecamp program is being rolled out to public schools without charge, just like Facebook is provided to users "without charge," critics raise privacy concerns because, like Facebook, Summit collects valuable user data, that is, student data.[25] The agreement between Summit and the participating school

25. See Faith Boninger, Alex Molnar, and Kevin Murray, "Asleep at the Switch: Schoolhouse Commercialism, Student Privacy, and the Failure of Policymaking," *National Education Policy Center,* August 2017, http://nepc.colorado.edu/publication/schoolhouse-commercialism-2017; see also Emma Brown and Todd C. Frankel, "Facebook Backed School Software Shows Promise and Raises Privacy Concerns," *Washington Post,* October 11,

states that Summit may use student data to develop educational services.[26] Since Summit is part of a for-profit company, CZI, LLC, this means that the data could be used to develop other for-profit educational services within CZI's umbrella. Facebook is an advertising company. Most of its profit comes from using volunteered data to sell ads targeting its users. A personalized learning curriculum sets the stage for a new kind of profit taking by educational investors in the form of data mining. Just as Facebook uses and sells data from its users to advertisers, the data that can be collected from a young school-based "captive audience" not in a position to refuse it could be worth a fortune.

CZI's private for-profit form and the interrelations of for-profit and nonprofit entities and sharing of commercializable information raise a number of troubling questions: Will CZI finance its educational activities through the commercialization of its users' data, as Facebook does? Will the content in Summit applications embed advertising? Will Summit deliver users to Facebook, which will deliver them to advertisers? Will Summit use taken data and put them through big data models to derive commercially valuable marketing information? There appears to be nothing in the user agreement or the laws structuring CZI as an LLC that would preclude these commercial possibilities. Moreover, due to the LLC form, one can never know the answers to these questions. Consequently, the public ought to assume that the answers to these questions are all yes unless proven otherwise.

The Cambridge Analytica scandal that emerged in 2018 revealed that as early as 2015, Facebook and Zuckerberg were aware that Cambridge Analytica was secretly taking Facebook users' data and using them to advertise political campaigns, such

---

2016, https://www.washingtonpost.com/local/education/facebook-backed
-school-software-shows-promise—and-raises-privacy-concerns/2016/10/11
/2580f9fe-80c6-11e6-b002-307601806392_story.html.

26. Summit's user agreement with schools is available at https://drive
.google.com/file/d/0B4_mvdmEmtsTYXF4M3RUb1hLalE/view.

as Trump's 2016 presidential campaign. The taking of 87 million people's data without their knowledge or consent to be used to manipulate them politically highlights more than the questionable judgment of CZI and Zuckerberg. It also showcases how private companies with a vested financial interest cannot be trusted to regulate themselves when it comes to the responsible use of private information. The Cambridge Analytica scandal shows that Zuckerberg, Facebook, and CZI ought to be forced to open Summit and all of CZI's activities to public accountability, oversight, and regulation or face expulsion from public schools to protect children's legal rights to privacy.

Among the most troubling aspects of CZI's expansion of Summit is the effort to replace teachers with machines and to shift the control over knowledge from teachers to a for-profit company. CZI has been promoting "personalized learning," "software that puts children in charge of their own learning, recasting their teachers as facilitators and mentors."[27] Zuckerberg has explained the vision for how personalized learning works in a classroom: "Students cluster together, working at laptops. They use software to select their own assignments, working at their own pace. And, should they struggle at teaching themselves, teachers are on hand to guide them."[28]

On the surface, this vision for personalized learning appears to counter some of the worst aspects of the past two decades of excessive standardized testing, the central feature of the so-called accountability movement. It replaces the single high-stakes test with the possibility of taking a test as many times as is necessary to check "mastery." However, rather than getting rid of the accountability movement's legacy of overtesting, which has been opposed by the antitesting Opt Out movement, Summit's program appears to build testing more deeply into the curriculum and worsens the

27. Natasha Singer, "The Silicon Valley Billionaires Remaking America's Schools," *New York Times,* June 6, 2017.

28. Singer.

problems of teaching to the test. Orienting learning around constant testing and teaching to the test displaces dialogue in favor of a monologic form of learning. Such a model of pedagogy displaces dialogue, curiosity, investigation, interpretation, judgment, and debate in favor of transmission through passive absorption. Moreover, standardized tests obscure the social and ideological positions of the makers of the tests and the takers of the tests. As a consequence, knowledge appears disconnected from its conditions of production and the symbolic and material contests that inform claims to truth.

CZI's expansion of standardized testing is more extensive than its integration into personalized learning. In spring 2017, CZI partnered with The College Board, which sells the PSAT, SAT, and Advanced Placement tests, to expand adaptive learning test preparation in school.[29] CZI does not appear to be committed to ending or replacing standardized testing as a gate to academic promotion and economic inclusion so much as it wants to enter into pay-for-fee services in an ever more competitive testing climate.

Proponents of personalized learning claim that in opposition to competitive individualized learning, personalized learning emphasizes collective learning with students clustered around tables together. Zuckerberg and Summit CEO Diane Tavenner liken this collective learning to the corporate culture of a tech company. According to Zuckerberg, "it feels like the future—it feels like a start up."[30] And says Tavenner, "It looks more like Google or Facebook than a school."[31] Empirical evidence of traditional measures of test-based achievement do not exist to support the claims of proponents of personalized learning. Such traditional measures of test-based achievement fail to address a

29. Gregg Toppo, "College Board, Zuckerberg Hope to Boost Access to College Partnership to Focus on Motivation and Student Achievement," *USA Today,* May 16, 2017, A3.

30. Singer, "Silicon Valley Billionaires."

31. Singer.

more significant matter that bears on the personalized learning debate, namely, how it impacts the ways that teachers and students address the politics of the curriculum—that is, contested knowledge and meanings and the ways that these contests are connected to broader material and symbolic struggles.

CZI's promotion of "personalized learning" aims to replace teachers with machines, to replace dialogue between teachers and students with student use of programmed software. It replaces the meaning-making work that teachers do in classrooms, which is often contextually based, with a decontextualized software program. Promoters of the software suggest that, by being adaptive to students, it is "responsive" and "relevant." Providence, Rhode Island, school superintendent Christopher Maher, who is overseeing one of the most extensive implementations of personalized learning with CZI, stated, "Personalized-learning technology helps students choose subjects they find personally meaningful and culturally relevant."[32] However, whereas teachers can link knowledge to student experience to make learning relevant, such software cannot. Furthermore, teachers can go beyond linking knowledge to experience by problematizing how knowledge is produced and how its production relates to the particular social environment experienced by the student. To give an example from Maher's district, how might a working-class student who is African American or Latino use personalized learning software to make sense of the experience of the extreme racial and class segregation that currently structures the city of Providence and the racialized and class-based pedagogies of repression that currently organize its public schools? Whereas a teacher can engage in dialogue with this student about the history of that reality, the competing ways of theorizing and interpreting that reality, the curriculum software cannot. As CZI moves to displace teachers

32. Tim Newcomb, "Will Personalized Learning Become the New Normal?," *The Atlantic,* March 29, 2017.

with technology, it repurposes teachers as "mentors." As mentors, teachers are not "deliverers of content" but rather take on the role of fostering "cognitive skills."[33] In CZI's vision, there is an artificial split introduced between "content" and "thinking," as if one can think without content.[34] As Paulo Freire emphasized, teachers are always more than facilitators or "mentors." A teacher's pedagogical authority is always exercised whether the teacher intervenes to question the content or silently affirms it and tacitly endorses it.

"Personalized learning" is not just a misnomer; it is an oxymoron in that it depersonalizes learning as it removes learning from the subjective realities of students' lives, the objective realities of the broader context for learning, and the dialogue between teachers and students. By depersonalizing learning, such software also denies the relationships between claims to truth and the ideological positions and social interests that often animate claims to truth. In this sense, CZI's educational activities run contrary to the aspirations of democratic education that aims to promote dispositions of curiosity, dissent, and dialogue and that links knowledge to power such that knowledge can form the basis for social agency. Instead of rewarding students with understanding their potential to act on the community and the world, personalized learning software often rewards learning with video game–style extrinsic rewards.

A key feature of "personalized learning" is what Garrison et al. has referred to as "the Netflixing of education," or the implementation of adaptive software and data analytics.[35] Adaptive

33. Chris Berdik, "Tipping Point: Can Summit Put Personalized Learning over the Top?," *The Hechinger Report,* January 17, 2017.

34. "Summit requires Basecamp schools to follow its practice of basing 30 percent of grades on mastery of content and 70 percent on students' use of various cognitive skills, such as making inferences and clearly communicating their ideas." Berdik.

35. Heather Roberts Mahoney, Alexander Means, and Mark Garrison, "Netflixing Human Capital Development: Personalized Learning

software works like Netflix to predict and suggest the direction of lessons. Data analytics compile and quantify the student's use of the software, measures her use with tests, and provides the teacher with data that are supposed to inform the teacher's mentorship. As I have discussed elsewhere,[36] the expansion of adaptive learning technology and its informatization is troubling because it provides a prescribed path of curriculum and creates a longitudinal case about the student over the course of a year and from year to year. Because the "data" about the student's activities are numerically quantified, these activities falsely appear as neutral and objective. As well, because the student chooses some activities and to some extent the pace of use, the program appears to foster individual control over learning despite the fact that the lessons are prefabricated and standardized. Adaptive learning software sorts and sifts students, promoting some and punishing others. Like standardized testing and the standardization of curriculum, such sorting and sifting are informed by a cultural politics that the software does not make explicit to its users. Hence the curriculum of adaptive learning software puts forward particular class and cultural group values, ideologies, and subject positions while falsely wrapping these cultural politics in a guise of disinterested universality and objectivity abetted by the ideology of technology.[37]

Personalized learning software recontextualizes knowledge in ways that are viscerally stimulating but remove the skill acquisition from any meaningful individual or social use. Take, for example, Netflix founder Reed Hastings's Dreambox Learning:

> Dreambox takes elements from animated video games, with some math lessons populated by aliens that whoosh and animals that

---

Technology and the Corporatization of K–12 Education," *Journal of Education Policy* 31, no. 4 (2016): 405–20.

36. Saltman, "Corporate Schooling Meets Corporate Media."

37. Algorithms are not neutral, point out Boninger et al., "Asleep at the Switch."

cluck. When students complete a math lesson successfully, they earn points that they can use to unlock virtual rewards.[38]

Learning math in this case becomes not about learning tools to understand the self and the social world to be able to act on it. Math in this case is a desocialized skill linked to meaningless extrinsic rewards and frivolous entertainment. The point is not that there is no place for frivolous entertainment but that the pedagogical approach favored by personalized learning disconnects skills from their social meanings and possibilities. Compare this Dreambox example to a lesson developed by critical math educators who, for example (to use a former Chicago colleague's lesson), teach Latinx youth fractions by doing driving while brown/driving while black lessons.[39] In this case, the experience of these youths being targeted by police was analyzed with fractions, furthering the comprehension of the experience. The lesson then became the basis for a community action project to challenge racist police practices. This example highlights the crucial difference between what relevant and meaningful learning can be about when contextualized socially and made relevant to the individual student experience.

There is a false debate found in both the popular and academic literature about personalized learning. Proponents, such as Maher, falsely portray it as relevant and meaningful while celebrating these supposed virtues against transmission models of pedagogy. Critics of personalized learning, such as Benjamin Riley, defend the role of teachers as imparters of knowledge that can be accumulated by students.[40] Both positions fail to comprehend the cultural politics of knowledge making in schools. Such proponents of personalized learning are now appropriating from traditions of

38. Singer, "Silicon Valley Billionaires."

39. This example comes from Eric Gutstein. See also the work of Mark Wolfmeyer, such as *Mathematics Education: A Critical Introduction* (New York: Routledge, 2017).

40. Newcomb, "Will Personalized Learning Become the New Normal?"

critical education the rhetoric of meaningful and relevant learning while promoting forms of learning that are neither. Personalized learning is depersonalized by decontextualizing knowledge from its conditions of formation. The transmission model that sees the teacher as imparter of knowledge treats knowledge as static and the student as an empty vessel. Both positions miss the way that knowledge is co-created through dialogic exchange between teachers and students. As Stuart Hall emphasizes, culture is made through meaning-making practices through exchange, albeit in always unequal ways.[41]

Pillaging Teacher Work for Profit

According to Dale Russakoff in *The Prize*, Zuckerberg's central focus on school reform in Newark involved changing teacher work. Russakoff writes that Zuckerberg saw the teacher workforce as a problem and was interested in making teaching work attractive. What Russakoff does not explain is why, then, Zuckerberg embraced neoliberal educational reforms that are thoroughly offputting to prospective teachers by transforming teaching from a profession with professional security, autonomy, and control over pedagogical and curricular decisions to an insecure job subject to intense surveillance, micromanagement, punishing testbased accountability, and downward pressure on pay and benefits. Specifically, Zuckerberg in Newark was onboard with Booker and Christie's push for union busting, chartering, and value-added modeling.

CZI continues Zuckerberg's long-standing focus on framing the teacher and teacher work as problems that need to be overcome. The different aspects of CZI's educational activities hinge on an allegation that teachers are "unaccountable" and need to be made accountable. This was evident in Zuckerberg's Newark activities

41. See, e.g., Stuart Hall, *Representation: Cultural Representations and Signifying Practices* (Thousand Oaks, Calif.: Sage, 1997).

that positioned the teacher workforce as both problem and solution. It is also evident in CZI's project of replacing teachers with machines. According to Zuckerberg, what will allegedly produce accountability is students' activities on the software, which can be numerically quantified and will represent real learning. Students are to be accountable to the software, which is made elsewhere by experts. Yet students are not to be accountable to the teachers who play a new role in CZI's vision no longer as teachers but as "mentors." As Zuckerberg's educational solutions demand numerically quantifiable accountability from his product, Zuckerberg's own educational activity has been and continues to be unaccountable to the public due to the secrecy afforded the LLC structure.

CZI's plan to replace teachers with a "student-centered" approach is not a new privatization strategy. When Chris Whittle announced his plans for the Edison Schools, now Edison Learning, a for-profit company that manages schools, he described a seemingly progressive vision in which fewer teachers could be used as students taught students. This labor and cost saving plan was soon enough scrapped by Whittle and replaced with a radically rigid and standardized approach that involved having every student in every Edison School learn the same thing at the same time. The earlier example of Edison is significant for how, in the history of corporate school reform, the celebration of student freedom from teachers has been about reducing the overhead of teacher labor to maximize profits by reducing the single biggest element of school overhead. In the case of CZI, the shift of money away from the teacher workforce and toward for-profit companies that develop curriculum software and adaptive learning technologies represents a redistribution of public wealth from public employees to private ones. It also represents a shift in control over who decides what should be taught and how it should be taught. The media scandal over Facebook's editorial role in overseeing its newsfeed following the 2016 presidential election has great relevance for this question of curricular control. Following the discovery that a large quantity of fake news stories during the 2016 presidential election were circulated through Facebook, the company's editorial oversight came under scrutiny. This scrutiny revealed that a small number of people at the company were making decisions about what news to send to users' Facebook pages. News, like curriculum, always comes from a particular vantage point with particular assumptions.

Personalized learning promoted by CZI denies and obscures the human and inherently political practices of meaning making by disappearing those making the curriculum and disallowing dialogue between students and those making claims to truth. In this sense, CZI's version of personalized learning is antithetical to democracy itself. Henry Giroux makes the point that education is always implicated in both politics and the kind of society people are collectively forming:

> Education [is] important not only for gainful employment but also for creating the formative culture of beliefs, practices, and social relations that enable individuals to wield power, learn how to govern, and nurture a democratic society that takes equality, justice, shared values, and freedom seriously.[42]

As CZI works rapidly to expand as an education business disguised as a philanthropy, citizens need to comprehend the broader social and political stakes in the expansion of standardized testing and standardized curriculum, destruction of the dialogic relationship between teachers and students, redistribution of educational resources, and decision-making about pedagogy and curriculum from the public and teachers to the corporation.

42. Henry A. Giroux, *On Critical Pedagogy* (New York: Continuum, 2011).

Charter School Real Estate Schemes and the Theft of Agency: Andre Agassi and the Celebrity Branding of Schools

IN HIS AUTOBIOGRAPHY, tennis star Andre Agassi revealed that his authoritarian father had stolen his childhood, his agency, and his education by forcing him to train to become a world champion athlete.[1] Putting him on a strict disciplinary training regimen, Agassi's father made him hit balls instead of going to school and later sent him away to a tennis academy that allowed him to effectively drop out of school by ninth grade. Agassi explains that his father terrorized him and his siblings with explosive anger while taking away any choice that he had to play a game he claims to have hated.

Not only did Agassi's father demand total obedience to authority but he also taught Agassi that thinking and questioning are to be avoided. Choice and control taken away, Agassi details how he expressed control through self-fashioning and regularly remaking his appearance and through alcohol and drug use. Andre's father, Mike, was a frustrated former champion boxer who didn't have the chance to compete at tennis, and so he attempted to make his children into world tennis champions, imposing his will, his dreams, and his desires on his children. As well, Mike Agassi saw his children as a potential big payout with prize money and endorsements. From the youngest age, Andre

1. Andre Agassi, *Open: An Autobiography* (New York: Viking Press, 2009).

was inserted not only into his father's dreams but also into his father's fantasy of transforming children into money. As Andre's older siblings failed to win trophies and prize money, the pressure mounted on the last hope. While Agassi reached the top of the game, winning prizes and numerous corporate endorsements, he details how the undermining of his agency resulted in feelings of anxiety, depression, alienation, and confusion about his own desires. In a somewhat predictable pattern for confessional autobiographies by celebrities, we learn that after a failed marriage and relationships, a stint with crystal meth, abuse of alcohol and toupees, and a turbulent career, Agassi found salvation. Salvation for Agassi came in finding love with another tennis star and in privatizing public schools—continuing the family tradition of making children into profit engines. Agassi was going to open a chain of charter schools, but following a string of scandals, he instead started a charter school facilities real estate investment company.[2]

This chapter shows how, in the absence of evidence and argument, faith in markets and a cult of personality play an outsized role in promoting the continued expansion of the charter movement. There are two primary motivations for charter school development that I explore here. One is the profit motive. The other is ideology. Neoliberal ideology has not only justified privatization, deregulation, and union busting but also driven the expansion of corporate culture, managerialism, and a revival of a positivist approach to knowledge. I am showing here how the profiteering of charter school real estate, bond, and other financial schemes has very much to do with an unexplored dimension of the ideology of corporate culture that is applied to school reform: the cult of personality in charter school promotion and the replacement of learning for social agency with mystified

2. Ruth Mccambridge, "Hedge Funds, Andre Agassi, and Charter Schools: Education Capitalism in Action," *Non-Profit Quarterly,* October 31, 2014.

forms of consumerist agency produced through the association of schools with celebrities.

In pointing out the role of culture, symbols, and spectacle in school reform, I am highlighting the extent to which the swindles of innovative educational finance depend on cultural ideologies that not only work in conjunction with profit motives but at times create the cultural conditions within which extraction of wealth from the public becomes intelligible as a course of action. The first section discusses the varieties of profit seeking in the charter movement, with particular attention to charter school real estate and municipal bond issuance. The second section explains how celebrities, often with no education themselves, become authorized to act as school reformers.

On one level, the simple explanation is that when education is turned into a market, anyone can become a player. However, celebrities in particular, without knowledge and experience of education, have been sought out to partner with other charter investors, as if being an athlete, rapper, or musician gives insight into curriculum, pedagogy, or administration. I contend that there is more at play than simply the attachment of a recognizable brand, such as Agassi, to a school in a market atmosphere. I explain that the legacy of positivist rationality that structures so much of contemporary educational thinking, especially standardized testing, estranges facts from the history and context of their making and meaning. This contemporary positivist alienation of fact contributes to antitheoretical and anti-intellectual culture that seeks explanations for social phenomena and grounding for educational policy not through recourse to evidence and argument but through reference to image, the body, and even the logic of conspiracy. I contend that educational profiteering needs to reckon with the contemporary epistemological crisis of truth and lies, fact and theory, and a growing turn to "superagents" and the cult of personality around them to anchor market-based projects that are otherwise unsupportable.

Charter Schools and the Pursuit of Profit

Forty-five percent of all charter enrollments are in educational management organizations, or EMOs. As of the 2014–15 academic year, for-profit EMOs "ran more than 900 charter or district schools across the U.S. and approximately 300 nonprofit EMOs operated more than 2000 charter schools."[3] In some states, the majority of charter schools are for-profit companies. For-profits predominate in Michigan (85 percent), Florida, Arizona, and Ohio.

As Baker and Miron explain, "most nonprofit EMOs look, act, and have management agreements similar to for-profit EMOs."[4] Common to both for-profits and nonprofits is that, on the whole, they have higher administrative costs (such as pay to owner/operators) and lower teacher pay than traditional public schools. Nonprofits are most common in Texas, Illinois, New York, and California.[5] While for-profits can legally extract money as profit and nonprofit charters must show that expenses go back into operations, the reality is that both for-profits and nonprofits create wealth for owners/operators in the same way, namely, by building expenses for administration into the justified expenditures. Sometimes these charter administrative salaries are enormous, and sometimes cronies and family members receive high salaries as administrators to keep the money flowing in. One high-profile "nonprofit" charter EMO in Chicago, named UNO, was discovered to be paying extraordinarily high administrative salaries to founder Juan Rangel and his family members (whose role in administration was unclear). The EMO was found to be contracting operations to itself.[6]

---

3. Bruce Baker and Gary Miron, "The Business of Charter Schooling: Understanding the Policies That Charter Operators Use for Financial Benefit," National Education Policy Center, December 10, 2015, http://nepc .colorado.edu/publication/charter-revenue, 8.

4. Baker and Miron, 7.

5. Baker and Miron, 8.

6. Dan Mihalopoulos and Paul Saltzman, "Tracking Charter Finance," *The IRE Journal,* Summer 2014, 20–22.

Because of the many possibilities for profit, not just hedge fund titans but movie theater companies, retired tennis stars, and other celebrities have rushed to become major investors in charter school facilities.[7] Charter school real estate companies often acquire school buildings cheaply from public districts. The real estate investors have a relationship with or serve on the boards of charter school management companies. Investors then lease the property to the charter school board at a large profit. The board therefore is practically leasing its own property to itself in the form of the charter school, for which they receive public money. As in the case of Andre Agassi and his partner Bryan Turner, the real estate investor acquires cheap property, leases it to himself as the charter founder, and extracts profit by taking a significant portion of the public tax money directed to fund the charter school for overhead.[8]

Charter school real estate investors in the United States like Turner and Agassi claim that only with the expansion of the profit motive in U.S. schooling can schools be improved. Investors and charter proponents claim that drawing private capital and profit motive into public schooling is mandatory. According to Turner, "if you want to treat a problem, then philanthropy is fine. But if you want to cure, really cure, you've got to harness market forces to create sustainable solutions that are scalable."[9] Turner and Agassi run two companies that invest in charter school real estate. They buy cheap property and lease it to the charter schools at high interest rates. Turner and Agassi's profit is coming from public wealth. Contrary to the picture Turner paints of an unfettered free market doing good, the profit-making enterprises Turner and

7. Alan Singer, "Why Rich Folks Love Charter Schools," *Seattle Education,* November 14, 2015.

8. Mccambridge, "Hedge Funds."

9. Paul Perry, "Is Impact Investment About to Turbo-Charge the Charter School Movement," *Inside Philanthropy,* August 29, 2016, https://www.insidephilanthropy.com/home/2016/8/29/is-impact-investing-about-to-turbo-charge-the-charter-school.html.

Agassi run rely on government regulations, laws, and tax incentives that create the conditions for their businesses.

As educational finance scholar Bruce Baker has detailed, the biggest loser in this charter school real estate leasing scenario is the public. The public pays first to build the school building, then gives it away and keeps paying for it to the private real estate investor who now owns it.[10] As Baker explains it, the public pays twice while losing the school. The charter school real estate investors make money by charging rents that often far exceed 20 percent.[11] They have also profited by getting New Market Tax Credits that from 2000 to 2014 publicly subsidized private investors to develop school facilities for charters.[12] These tax credits allowed investors to double their money in seven years.[13]

Large profits in charter school real estate also include the issuance of charter municipal bonds. From 1998 to 2017, more than one thousand tax-exempt charter municipal bonds have been issued, representing at least $15.5 billion in debt.[14] Charter schools

10. Bruce D. Baker of Rutgers University is a leading scholar of school finance. In addition to his scholarly journal articles, his blogs are a crucial resource. He blogs at *School Finance 101*. See Baker, "We Bought It Twice but We No Longer Own It: The Bad Public Policy behind Charter School Real Estate Deals," *School Finance 101* (blog), July 21, 2015, https://schoolfinance101.wordpress.com/2015/07/21/we-bought-it-twice-but-we-no-longer-own-it-is-co-location-the-better-option/.

11. Kristin Rawls, "Who Is Profiting from Charters? The Big Bucks behind Charter School Secrecy, Financial Scandal and Corruption," Alternet, May 8, 2013, https://www.alternet.org/education/who-profiting-charters-big-bucks-behind-charter-school-secrecy-financial-scandal-and.

12. Strauss, "Why Hedge Funds Love Charter Schools."

13. See Wiggin, "Charter School Gravy Train"; Singer, "Why Rich Folks Love Charter Schools"; Strauss, "Why Hedge Funds Love Charter Schools"; and A. D. Pruitt, "Entertainment REIT in Trouble at School—Theater Landlord's Push into the Education Business Hits a Snag; CEO Says He Has Learned Several Important Lessons," *Wall Street Journal,* June 27, 2012, C8.

14. Reuters, "Number of Charter Schools, Students in U.S. Rises: Report," August 22, 2017, https://www.reuters.com/article/us-education-charterschools/number-of-charter-schools-students-in-u-s-rises-report-idUSKCN1B22JX.

are risky because they can so easily fail or face financial difficulties; this makes charter municipal bond investments in turn risky.[15] Yet, in states with some of the highest concentration of for-profit charter schools, these bonds are insured by public funds.[16] Baker calls this scenario "subprime chartering," warning of a massive charter municipal bond bubble that could burst with dire impact for the rest of the economy.[17] With the public holding the bag, the bursting of this education finance bubble would result in the public bailing out the private sector just as it did in the subprime mortgage crash of 2008. While the $1.3 trillion student loan debt bubble is now well known to the public, the charter municipal debt bubble that could rival it remains largely unknown.

Agassi has received media attention and criticism as a major investor in charter school facilities development.[18] Some criticism has highlighted how he has profited massively from these investments; yet, in terms of test-based student achievement, the charters he has opened have fared poorly, among the worst for Las Vegas–area public schools.[19] It is difficult to justify the draining of public money from the public school system under the auspices of private-sector "impact investing" alleged to be necessary to keep the charter movement expanding.

Since the late 1990s, the charter movement has been hamstrung by the fact that facilities are not typically provided by school districts. Under the Clinton administration, New Market Tax Credits

15. Aaron Kuriloff, "Charter Schools Find Smarter Way to Borrow," *Wall Street Journal,* December 28, 2014, 1.

16. PRNewswire, "Creative State Programs Help Charter Schools Shift Millions of Dollars to Core Education Needs as They Build and Expand, Says New National Study," July 22, 2015.

17. Bruce D. Baker, "Picture Post Week: Subprime Chartering," *School Finance 101* (blog), December 10, 2015, https://schoolfinance101.wordpress .com/2015/12/10/picture-post-week-subprime-chartering/.

18. Mccambridge, "Hedge Funds."

19. Diane Ravitch discusses this briefly in *Reign of Error* (New York: Knopf, 2013).

were launched to incentivize private investors to develop school facilities.[20] The charter movement was premised on a business language and logic that called for greater market competition paired with consumer choice, market accountability, and concentrated leadership power by deregulating control by communities, teachers, and their unions. "Just like in markets," the competition and choice were supposed to put pressure on all schools to improve quality as they competed for students and tax dollars. While there is no evidence to suggest that this vision came to fruition,[21] this did not slow the expansion of the charter movement. Even as empirical evidence for test score improvement was lacking and a number of problems with chartering became empirically established (including pushouts, worsened racial segregation, suppressed pay and security for teachers as administrative costs ballooned[22]), venture philanthropists poured billions of dollars into expanding the charter movement.[23] Not only did educational researchers point to the lack of evidence of success on the terms that charter boosters had predicted but even the business press recognized just how lackluster charter performance had been. By 2013, the business press was citing educational research studies of the failures to beat public schools in terms of test scores and

20. Darcia Harris Bowman, "Charters Hit by Facilities Funding Woes," *Education Week,* November 8, 2000, 1.

21. On evidence that competition pressure does not benefit public schooling, see, e.g., the work of Sharon Nichols, David Berliner, and Gene Glass, "High Stakes Testing and Student Achievement: Does Accountability Pressure Increase Student Learning?," *Education Policy Analysis Archives* 14 (2006), https://epaa.asu.edu/ojs/article/view/72.

22. I review these studies in Saltman, *Failure of Corporate School Reform.*

23. Juan Gonzalez, "Hedge Fund Execs' Money for Charter Schools May Pay Off," *New York Daily News,* March 11, 2015, and Paul Perry, "A Building Boom for Charter Schools Is Coming. Guess Who's Footing the Bill?," Inside Philanthropy, August 9, 2016, https://www.insidephilanthropy.com/charter-schools/2016/8/9/a-building-boom-for-charter-schools-is-coming-guess-whos-foo.html.

efficient spending despite charters' capacity to cherry-pick students.[24] Nonetheless, as *Forbes* pointed out, the business press recognized just how lucrative charter schooling is for investors like Agassi, in large part due to public subsidies in the form of New Market Tax Credits.[25]

Ideological Motivations for Charter Expansion

The charter school movement has continued to expand in the United States. While charter schools compose only approximately 6 percent of U.S. public schools, the charter school movement has worked feverishly to change state laws and lift caps on the number of charters. Superrich individuals and corporate philanthropies, such as the Walton Family Foundation (Walmart money), the Bill and Melinda Gates Foundation (Microsoft money), and the J. P. Morgan Chase Foundation, have financially backed the charter school movement.

Most of the people who are involved in the charter school movement are motivated less by personal financial profit than by ideological convictions. These ideological convictions hold that public schools are "failing," that the "discipline of markets" needs to be injected into the hopelessly bureaucratic public sector, that unions only protect lazy or incompetent teachers who are the cause of educational failure, that parents and students need to be seen as consumers given an educational "choice," and that the competition that they do as consumers will necessarily promote the magic of the market, with its efficiency, quality, and accountability. This ideological view has been steadily and systematically promoted in the last thirty years to the point that it is now largely common sense. Ideology stands in for the abundant empirical evidence for profound problems with chartering. These problems include

24. Wiggin, "Charter School Gravy Train."
25. Wiggin.

draining money from public schools; worsening racial segregation; pushing out special education students, English language learners, and students with discipline problems; inflating administrative pay while reducing teacher pay; failing to improve traditional measures of test-based achievement and emphasizing such positivist forms of assessment to guide pedagogy and curriculum rather than socially engaged and critical forms of education; tending to embrace repressive pedagogical approaches that aim more for control of bodies than intellectual stimulation; and busting unions, thereby making teaching precarious and underpaid work.

The first promise of charter schooling, when it was promoted by Albert Shanker and the American Federation of Teachers, was that it would provide innovative, alternative, and independent school models that would foster teacher autonomy. By the 1990s, chartering was hijacked by corporate reformers and venture philanthropists focused on test-based accountability and the possibilities of experimentation to discover the most efficacious models that would raise test scores. These corporate reformers revived the mid-twentieth-century promises of industrial efficiency, scientific management, and a transmission model of schooling. In this vision, schools promoting higher scores would be replicated and scaled up, and schools that did not would be "allowed to fail." Other corporate reformers, such as Andy Smarick, made it clear that charter expansion should be promoted in the short run to close traditional public schools and set the stage for declaring charters a failed experiment that would allow for opening a system of private, for-profit schooling nationwide.[26]

By about 2010, a number of evaluations had made it clear that the promise of raising test scores through chartering was a false promise as charters schools appeared to score about the same or worse on tests. So proponents like the Gates Foundation changed

26. Andy Smarick, "The Turnaround Fallacy: Stop Trying to Fix Failing Schools. Close Them and Start Fresh," *Education Next* 10, no. 1 (2010), http://educationnext.org/the-turnaround-fallacy/.

the criteria for success yet again. Instead of promising raised test scores, now charter expansion would facilitate "college and career readiness." For proponents of charter expansion, one virtue of this new benchmark for charters would be that, unlike test scores, university enrollment is not measured in a centralized way by the Department of Education. Consequently, it is extremely difficult to measure whether charter schooling as a reform collectively promotes "college and career readiness" more than, say, putting the forgone public resources into traditional public schools. Abundantly clear is that, absent evidence, faith in markets or market fundamentalism is what anchors privatization schemes, such as charters, in place of evidence for social benefit.

Charter School Investors, the Cult of Personality, and the Theft of Agency

In *Open,* Agassi repeats the standard tropes about the virtue of charter schools: they are deregulated and hence free of the constraints of public bureaucracy by being under the control of administrators. Agassi, scathingly critical of his own subjection to authoritarian control by his father and, later, his tennis academy coach, nonetheless promotes school reforms for their capacity to give unchecked control to a leader. Agassi repeatedly addresses what he calls the "contradiction" of a school dropout, such as him, becoming a school reform figure, suggesting that by confronting and embracing one's contradictions, one can live a more honest and better life. Agassi does not, however, address how this particular contradiction has implications for students attending a school designed by a person with no education in or knowledge of educational theory, curriculum studies, or pedagogy. Nor does Agassi explain his charter schools' school-to-work educational model. By mandating that kids need to work hard in school to succeed in the workforce, Agassi contradicts his own financial success, which resulted from his abandonment of school in favor of professional sports and celebrity endorsement. Is not Agassi's "do as I say, not as I do" perspective as much an authoritarian presumption as his de-democratizing efforts of facilitating charter schools that have privatized control?

One might interpret Agassi's educational activities as a classic case of psychological projection. He was subject to authoritarian control by parents and school. He dropped out of school, rejecting that control. He turned to a form of school reform that concentrated the control of the school, allowing economic elites to usurp the collective decision of the public. The school model that Agassi embraced tends toward repressive, if not authoritarian, pedagogies.[27] As a child, Agassi was treated as an object, a money machine, and as an adult, he treats children as objects, money machines for his real estate business.

Such an interpretation aligns with Paulo Freire and Erich Fromm's social psychological description of sadism, namely, the transformation of the other into an object of control.[28] Such objectification and instrumentalization of the other turn the other

27. The tendency of charters to have repressive pedagogical models relates to the fact that charters target working-class and poor nonwhite communities. Charters make the most inroads into communities that have historically suffered the worst public disinvestment and can't get a foot in the door in rich communities with lavishly funded public schools. The repressive pedagogies characteristic of charters are implicated in social and cultural reproduction—in producing different subjects with different dispositions for their future expected place in the economy. Studies in post-Katrina New Orleans's four charter networks confirm this, showing that the pedagogical approaches correspond to the class positions of the students. See Frank Adamson, Channa Cook-Harvey, and Linda Darling-Hammond, "Whose Choice? Student Experiences and Outcomes in the New Orleans School Marketplace," SCOPE Research Brief, September 2015, https://edpolicy.stanford.edu/sites/default/files/publications/scope-brief-student-experiencesneworleans.pdf. I discuss recent turns toward repressive pedagogy and the implication of the charter movement and privatization in it in Kenneth Saltman, *Scripted Bodies: Corporate Power, Smart Technologies, and the Undoing of Public Education* (New York: Routledge, 2016).

28. Freire, *Pedagogy of the Oppressed*; Erich Fromm, *Escape from Freedom* (New York: Holt, 1941).

into a dead thing, robbing one's victim of his subjectivity and humanity. The oppressed, Freire observes, suffer from "adhesion." That is, they learn to see freedom only as the power to oppress others, treat others as objects of control. In such a view, objectified and instrumentalized as a child, Agassi in turn grows up to objectify and instrumentalize children (respectively, through disciplinary repressive pedagogies and curriculum and through draining the public school system of resources to make real estate profits). Alternatively, one might interpret Agassi's educational activities as an extension of his expressed hatred of school and a form of deep cynicism about schooling. Profiting from school reform would not only further enrich him but would allow him to overcome bad press generated by his drug use, failed marriage, and regular jousting with sports reporters. This interpretation fits with his self-description as a Vegas kid reared on hustling as well as his shrewd activities as a businessman.

While there may be something to these interpretations, I want to focus on how a professional athlete and celebrity with no formal education can be taken seriously as an educational reformer and what that means for student agency. How does the attachment of Agassi's image to charter school development projects lend credibility and legitimacy rather than undermining credibility and legitimacy? What does this suggest about the dominant justification for charter expansion of "college and career readiness"? The answers to these questions lie in decades of ideological shifts that involve the meanings of school reform, the alienation of knowledge from evidence and argument, and the meanings of celebrity.

As a tennis star, Agassi endorsed Canon cameras. The advertising slogan featuring Agassi was "Image is everything." In *Open,* Agassi expresses frustration for how the media criticized him for an advertising campaign not of his own making. The press criticized him for his flamboyance and allegedly excessive attention to appearance as well as his transgressive aesthetic. Celebrity image is a kind of currency—symbolic currency that, like money, grants credibility in various domains.

As public schooling has become remade since the 1980s in the service of the private sector and itself as business, businesspeople are increasingly legitimated as government actors and, more particularly, as education reformers. There was a steady stream of rhetoric of the need for a businessperson to run inefficient public-sector bureaucracy to apply the discipline, competitiveness, and quantitative analysis of the realm of money. Upon his release from prison in the late 1990s, junk bond financier and felonious fraudster Michael Milken was redeemed by the media after he was barred from trading as he turned to educational privatization and building an education conglomerate.[29]

This logic has been transformed. Having money proves the capacity of a person to manage a public enterprise, even without business expertise. (Trump's secretary of education, Betsy Devos, is perhaps the clearest example of this.) What has developed out of this and reality television and social media is the increasing legitimation of imagery as capacity. Since the 1990s, reality stars who are famous for being famous are able to forge themselves into brands, translating image recognition into commercial endorsement potential (a good example of this is Paris Hilton).[30] These brands have financial value, endorsement value. Notoriety functions as symbolic wealth. The renown conveys legitimacy and credibility. An economy increasingly organized around click-through profits, advertising revenue measured by eyeballs on screens, and the commercialization of data amplifies notoriety as value. Agassi is hardly alone as a celebrity endorser of a public school that is positioned as a corporate product.

The rapper Pitbull, the musician John Legend, and the music producer Diddy, among others, have also gotten in on the game

29. Kathleen Morris, "The Reincarnation of Mike Milken," *Businessweek,* May 10, 1999; Kenneth Saltman, "Junk King Education," *Cultural Studies* 16, no. 2 (2002): 233–58.

30. See Henry Giroux, *Against the Terror of Neoliberalism* (New York: Routledge, 2015).

of charters. Pitbull (Armando Christian Perez) completed high school and partners with a large for-profit charter management company, Academica, as an investor in the Sports Leadership and Management charter school in Miami. Despite his lack of advanced formal education and his urban outlaw image, his financial success as a popular rapper and commercial product endorser make him a legitimate figure for the school reform business.

Unlike Agassi and Pitbull, John Legend received an Ivy League university education and worked for a major corporate consulting firm, Boston Consulting Group, before becoming a celebrity. Since becoming a celebrity, he has been active in several corporate school reform organizations dedicated to privatization and union busting, including Stand for Children and Teach for America. Legend, who is African American, in 2016 denounced the NAACP's call for a moratorium on charter schools.[31] The NAACP's moratorium was based in empirical studies, including findings of their own research task force, that showed chartering as exacerbating rather than reducing racial segregation in public schools.[32] Legend's advocacy of charters and privatization is not based on exhaustive research and a commitment against racial segregation and the erosion of public schooling the way that the NAACP position is. Rather, Legend puts his faith in a market-based consumer choice model for public school enrollments. Legend, despite having only an undergraduate degree, was, because of his fame, invited to serve on the board of trustees for the University of Pennsylvania Law School's Quattrone Center for the Fair Administration of Justice. The Quattrone Center makes compiling data and conducting empirical analysis for criminal justice reform central to its work. Yet, as Jose Luis Vilson observes, education does not merit the same

31. Coverage of Legend's response is available at http://www.essence
.com/news/john-legend-charter-public-schools-naacp.

32. The NAACP position on charter schools and their research can be accessed at http://www.naacp.org/campaigns/naacp-plan-action-charter
-schools/.

treatment from Legend.[33] The university promoted this celebrity appointment on its website.

Rapper, music producer, and alcoholic beverage entrepreneur Sean "Diddy" Combs became famous as much through his music as for his notorious association with the East Coast–West Coast gangster rap feud that resulted in the deaths of Tupac Shakur and Notorious BIG in the 1990s. Combs, in 2016, started a Harlem charter school that features a website with the rap star surrounded by adoring children. Combs's school was designed by a proprivatization ideologue who has been accused of embellishing the record of his Hartford charter school and who describes himself as a "brand."[34] The point not to be missed about the relatively recent rise of celebrity associations and endorsements of educational privatization is that, in the absence of evidence for the social and educational value of charter expansion, celebrity branding has taken on a significant symbolic role.

Celebrity endorsements and investments for educational privatization on the surface seem preposterous. After all, as Vilson points out, why would educational quality be enhanced by affiliation with athletes and musicians who themselves either have little education or lack any background, expertise, or familiarity in educational policy, planning, research, or curriculum theory? The simple answer is that it is not enhanced.

---

33. See education author Jose Luis Vilson's insightful blog post about John Legend's corporatist advocacy and how only in education can celebrity voices drown out informed policy and research, "John Legend and the Well-Meaning Corporatists," *JLV* (blog), March 13, 2013, http://thejosevilson.com/john-legend-and-the-well-meaning-corporatists/.

34. Diddy designed his school with a relentlessly self-promoting educational privatization and union-busting television personality who goes by "Dr. Steve Perry." Dr. Perry, who has been subject to numerous calls for investigation, received his doctorate in education at the University of Hartford, where his dissertation was directed by an adjunct. http://wnpr.org/post/hartford-board-education-chairman-calls-investigation-principal-steve-perry; http://citylimits.org/2015/03/13/hartford-to-harlem-charter-school-faces-critics-back-home/.

Yet it is done for several reasons. In a cultural and political context in which the public is increasingly framed as the private sector and schools are positioned not as public institutions but as businesses, a commercial logic deepens. Like the marketing of any commodity, association with a celebrity endorsement sells products. Charter schools must compete for students and, with funding dependent on enrollments, market their brand to prospective students and families. The dirty underside of what proponents celebrate as market-style "competition" is that charters spend a portion of funds that would otherwise pay for educational resources on advertising, marketing, and promotions to lure prospective students and parents. This is one high cost of John Legend's beloved "consumer choice." Celebrity attachments that otherwise should have no real connection to the school should be thought of as yet another cost of the logic of school competition. Schools are burdened not just with the material drain of the cost of promotion but with the symbolic drain of being associated with meanings that would not be acceptable by professional and ruling-class communities. Would gangster rappers and uneducated tennis players, whose successes are defined by the body and not the mind, be readily embraced as symbols by, for example, schools in the rich, predominantly white suburbs of major cities?

There is a seemingly contradictory connection of figures who have made a lot of money through exceptional industries like athletics and entertainment to schools saturated with ideologies about school as the path to jobs and security for working-class and poor students of color. What is not at all contradictory, however, is the long racist legacy of ascribing to black and brown youths the promise of corporeal forms of opportunity that affirm a racialized mind–body split that attributes intellect to whiteness and to nonwhites attributes of bodily capacity.[35]

The early millennial celebrity image from sports and enter-

35. See Hall, *Representation*; Herman Grey, *Watching Race: Television and the Struggle for Blackness* (Minneapolis: University of Minnesota Press, 2004).

tainment as symbolic currency represents a departure from the late 1990s trend of installing generals and military leaders in urban schools as a symbol of necessary discipline.[36] While the militarization of schools has steadily expanded and come to intersect with the charter movement,[37] the commercialization of schools through branding and celebrity represents a few key ideological shifts.

Agassi is used as a symbol of bootstrap hardscrabble grit, competition, and the financial success of someone who made it without education. This image fosters the central metaphor of charter promoters that charters inject private sector–style competition into the bloated bureaucratic public sector.

The charter movement in rhetoric fosters the development of independent and alternative school models. Yet, in reality, school development is highly limited by school founders' access to capital. For this reason, large corporate foundations, charter management organizations, and educational management organizations with a relatively homogenous ideological perspective emphasizing school-to-work and the ideologies of corporate culture have managed to expand.[38] More socially progressive and academic models that make learning the basis for interpretation and social intervention, or that have deeply democratic connections to community, tend not to find capital.

Democracy Prep

At the American Educational Research Association conference of 2017, a group of scholars from the Paulo Freire Democratic Project, affiliated with Chapman University in Orange, California (many of whom worked with Paulo Freire himself), detailed

---

36. See Saltman, *Collateral Damage.*

37. Nicole Nguyen, *A Curriculum of Fear: Homeland Security in U.S. Public Schools* (Minneapolis: University of Minnesota Press, 2016).

38. Saltman, *Gift of Education.*

their ten-year saga to secure funding for a charter school based in the liberatory pedagogy of Freire. Freire is widely considered to be among the most influential educational philosophers of the past century. The project aims to create the school in a predominantly working-class and poor Mexican American community in Santa Ana. Drawing on Freire's thought, the school would give students the intellectual tools to analyze self, society, and claims to truth and link learning to socially just community transformation. The project would also be linked to already existing community support projects, including early childhood education and adult literacy. The scholars recounted how the rightist Walton Family Foundation (Walmart money), a foundation known for its promotion of privatization and authoritarian leadership models, offered to fund the project on the condition that it determine the leadership of the school. The project organizers rejected this proposal and continue to search for funding.

Contrast the case of the Freire Democracy Project's longstanding inability to get charter funding to Democracy Prep, the charter outfit that bought Andre Agassi's charter school in Las Vegas. After being plagued by poor test-based performance and accusations of mismanagement, Agassi offloaded management of his academy to Democracy Prep. A nonprofit charter management organization, Democracy Prep was founded by Seth Andrews. Democracy Prep bills itself as centrally defined by civic engagement. However, its version of civic engagement, celebrated by the right-wing AEI, appears to limit the conception of civic engagement to the formal political process; delinks it from the specificities of community context; and voids civic engagement of the structural forces, such as class, gender, and race, that produce political subjects and contexts.[39] Central

39. See Daniel Lautzenheiser and Andrew Kelly, "Charter Schools as Nation Builders," AEI Program on American Citizenship Policy Brief 4, January 2013, http://www.aei.org/wp-content/uploads/2013/01/-charter-schools-as -nation-builders-democracy-prep-and-civic-education_155611749016.pdf.

community activities for the charter students involve get-out-the-vote demonstrations and participation in lobbying for charter expansion. For a school that is serving predominantly African American students, the curriculum appears not only to evacuate study of African American culture, struggle, history, and theory but also to impose the study of the Korean language. This appears to be because the founder taught English in Korea. My point is not that there is no value in studying Korean. What is significant is not only that the subjectivities, histories, contexts, and cultures of students are not taken up in relation to the curriculum in Democracy Prep's model but also that a seemingly arbitrary language and culture are imposed on students by the charter founder. A democratic pedagogy ideally would link learning to the process of interpreting and comprehending the social world students inhabit and interpreting the ways the self is formed by that social world.

Cults of personality allow the interests, whims, or quirks of the personality to be supported or to hold sway. The imposition of the interests or whims of the charter founder appears widespread. Andrews taught in Korea, so working-class African American U.S. students apparently have to learn Korean in high school. The rapper Pitbull likes sports, so he started a sports-themed charter. The music producers Jimmy Iovine and Andre Young (Dr. Dre), both of whom do not have university degrees, are financially successful in the music business, so they gave $70 million to the University of Southern California to start a music entrepreneurship academy that includes a high school program.

Pierre Bourdieu's conception of cultural capital as a form of social and symbolic wealth that is unequally distributed provides two distinct insights into the phenomenon of celebrity image that is attached to privatized schools. In "The Logic of Capital," Bourdieu explains the inverse relationship between the transmission of class status through monetary capital and cultural capital. For Bourdieu, cultural capital refers to socially valued knowledge, tastes, and dispositions and the means of acquiring them. Schools reproduce the class structure in part by unequally distributing cultural capital. Ruling- and professional-class students learn the language, codes, and tastes of power in the home, and the school largely rewards the cultural capital brought from home while adding to it. Working-class and poor students are punished in school for their knowledge, tastes, and dispositions. Grades and tests reward and punish students, making it seem as if the unequal distribution of cultural capital is based in merit, talent, and hard work rather than class origin.

In terms of Bourdieu's explanation of cultural capital as a means for the maintenance of the class structure, the attachment of the symbols of nonacademic competition, such as athletes and pop stars, does not represent a break with the actual pedagogies, curriculum, or models that these schools foist on students. That is, these schools distribute what passes as professional- and ruling-class cultural capital as universally valuable, neutral, and objective while punishing working-class cultural capital. At the same time, the highly rigid, standardized, decontextualized, and test-heavy forms of teaching in most charters represent pedagogies of obedience antithetical to intellectual dispositions for questioning, dialogue, and dissent. The disposition for obedience to authority and the treatment of knowledge as a deliverable gift from "those who know" represent the production of docile subjects in preparation for the low-pay, low-skill segment of the economy or worse and the making of subjects without the intellectual tools for collective self-defense. Yet these anti-intellectual schools attach symbols of corporeal working-class success (athletes, musicians, celebrities) to the educational machinery of symbolic violence. These symbols of working-class success exchanged the symbolic capital of the body for monetary capital. These athletes, musicians, and celebrities succeeded in the market despite their lack of school success and stand as symbols not of academic excellence but of the promise of individual talent actualized in the market. Some of the celebrity personalities, such as Agassi, preach hard work as the route to success even as their own hard work was not expressed academically. For a generation witnessing unprecedented concentrations of wealth, precarity, and downward mobility for everyone but the superrich, the spectacular success embodied by these figures represents both a false promise of academic meritocratic mobility and a mystification of the means by which wealth is produced. These schools offer students no intellectual tools to theorize the difference between working-class knowledge and culture of the family, the community, and the body as distinct from the professional class–based knowledge and culture of the school that circulates in institutions of power. While many of these schools aim to get students into university, and many do, the vast majority of students who attended charters drop out of university.[40] These students are largely unprepared to negotiate the intensified demands for professional-class cultural capital in universities that the schools do not give, nor are students prepared to approach knowledge as a means of social and political agency rather than a meaningless commodity to be consumed and exchanged.

Yet Bourdieu also explains that the function and significance of cultural capital declines as economic capital transmission becomes the more pronounced form for the reproduction of class.[41] In the past three decades, as income inequality has reached new heights and wealth has become radically concentrated in the hands of a few, the heritability of class dominance has become more directly economic and less cultural. Upward mobility has drastically declined, and education as a means of upward mobility

40. About 23 percent of charter school students complete a four-year university program. See the National Student Clearinghouse Research Center report *High School Benchmarks 2015: National College Progression Rates,* https://nscresearchcenter.org/hsbenchmarks2015/. This contrasts with a 59 percent four-year completion rate for U.S. students overall, according to the National Center for Educational Statistics report *Graduation Rates for Selected Cohorts* at https://nces.ed.gov/pubs2017/2017084.pdf.

41. Pierre Bourdieu, "The Forms of Capital," in *Handbook of Theory and Research for the Sociology of Education,* ed. J. Richardson, trans. Richard Nice, 46–58 (New York: Greenwood, 1986).

has also declined. Yet the ideology of educationally based merito-cratic climbing is omnipresent. As cultural capital declines in its significance as an equalizing force, education and culture become less important as transmitters of class power.

In such a context, money itself takes a more pronounced sym-bolic value as legitimator that can translate into multiple so-cial scenes. To have money confers legitimacy to make claims to knowledge. A president can be elected who has no experience in government but allegedly has a lot of money and a famous brand. A secretary of education can be appointed who has no experience in public schooling but is a billionaire intent on converting schools into businesses. An athlete or entertainer with no education can start schools. To have celebrity, to be a brand, confers legitimacy, because it represents a form of financially exchangeable symbolic power—a subjectified form of money. A president can be elected who has no experience in public service, and makes nothing, but licenses a brand image to be attached to various unrelated prod-ucts: reality television programs, steaks, beauty contests, neckties, buildings, a for-profit university

The attachment of seemingly incongruous figures like ten-nis stars and rappers to charter schools has another dimen-sion related to both contemporary politics and corporate school reform—the replacement of theory and arguments with the false foundation of numbers and essentialized identity. Contemporary politics has been formed through an antipathy to theory that in part derives from the legacy of positivism in knowledge-making domains. As education and journalism embrace a postpolitical pseudo-objectivism, they deny framing assumptions, values, and ideologies. In education, the standards and standardized test-ing movements have been joined by efforts to remove social jus-tice and theoretical subjects from teacher preparation programs. Objectivity and neutrality have been promoted under the guise of delivering ideological neutral "content," as if truth claims do not come from particular people with class and cultural locations. The decline of the power of cultural capital and the inflated value of financial capital as the preserve of class coincide with a two-decades-long educational accountability movement in which teaching to tests has become the norm. Standardized testing not only decontextualizes knowledge, removing it from its social conditions of formation; it also equates knowledge with authority. What is on the test appears legitimate because it has been deemed of value by experts elsewhere with power. Those with the power to claim the authority of standardized knowledge are not subject to questioning, identification, or dialogue.

A number of fields are undergoing a contradictory relationship with empirical data. On one hand, the investors profit from charter schooling and justify the profit as a benefit to the education system. Evidence suggests that this is decidedly not the case. The claim to financial efficacy is grounded not in evidence of benefit to the schools or the students but rather in brand image and the regurgitation of market ideologies of competition, choice, privatization, and deregulation invoked by the celebrity images. Even as there is no evidence that would justify the privatizations, recourse to empiricism is invoked to justify reforms that function in the interest of profit yet erode certain quality. For example, the charter movement dumps the standardized test score as the arbiter of quality and a backlash grows against the standardization of curriculum. Nonetheless, heavy standardized testing remains, and the charter movement continues to expand. Similarly, teachers are subject to value-added measures in which their positions are made insecure and measured by students' standardized test scores, or teachers are replaced with technology, such as personalized learning, that is falsely portrayed as objective, ideologically neutral, and universally valuable, even as it is misleadingly positioned as "personal" and "culturally responsive." These examples reveal that positivist ideology continues in educational reform to deny the values, assumptions, and ideologies behind claims to truth. Positivism rejects the relationship between theory and practice, eliding the theoretical assumptions behind practices. On one hand, fact is celebrated, and on the other hand, it appears to be suspect, free of context, history, and origins in human thought. In such a context, fact appears grounded by assertion, more specifically, by the assertion of people and institutions with unquestionable authority. Fact has been positioned as an alien enemy that comes from nowhere.

In the age of the suspicious fact unmoored from argument, evidence, and history, conspiracy grows. Vaccine conspiracies, chemtrails in the sky, birther conspiracy, the revival of age-old racist conspiracies about foreigners and enemies within—conspiratorial thought presumes that agency is dominated by those with secret control over knowledge and hence secret action. Absent theory, concept, or argument to explain social and individual realities, the logic of conspiracy finds foundational explanations in the essence of groups of people.[42] For conspiratorial thought, there are superagents who have a kind of magical capacity for understanding and action that is unique, exceptional, and beyond the usual rules of the game. Celebrity figures who attain top success in sports and entertainment typically do so outside of the meritocratic school ideology that promises that hard work in school results in economic success. Rather, such athletes and entertainers appear as exceptional products of talent or iron will. Attached to schools, the success of these celebrities is typically treated as magic and removed from the history and context that made it possible. Celebrities are alienated social facts. They appear as exceptionally powerful and capable, able to transcend the standard rules and formulas for economic rewards. As points of identification, celebrities represent to youth an impossible superagency that stands outside and against academic knowledge and its promise of economic inclusion.

As a symbol attached to charter schools, celebrity image functions to affirm a broad hostility to critical and public forms of

42. Angela Nagle, *Kill All Normies* (Washington, D.C.: Zero Books, 2017).

teaching and learning that would examine the values, assumptions, ideologies, and material and symbolic interests that often undergird claims to truth. There are many scholars of critical pedagogy and critical media literacy who take hip-hop, sports, and other popular cultural forms seriously and make them the basis for learning that is meaningful so that learning may become critical and socially transformative. However, these celebrity symbols attached to charter schools are not there in conjunction with critical pedagogies. They are attached, rather, to schools with largely repressive pedagogies that emphasize learning that is decontextualized from social contexts and student subjectivities. In this sense, the celebrity figures attached to charters function to give a guise of relevancy even as the model of the school provides no means for learning to be a source of social agency.

In contrast to celebrity superagents held out to them as promise, students in celebrity-branded charter schools are largely positioned as nonagents or spectatorial agents who are being educated to think of knowledge as at best a kind of cash currency that does not provide self- and social-explanatory power and, at worst, is just an irrelevant imposition by those with authority. Is this not the entire implicit point of the standardized test? Knowledge is made elsewhere; knowledge has nothing to do with the world; knowledge provides no insights into the self; knowledge has nothing to do with the context; knowledge has nothing to do with agency other than as an alienated thing to acquire, display, exchange. In the absence of knowledge and learning as providers of meaning and agency, the celebrity superagent attached to the school offers a different promise of agency, agency that comes from the body itself. Yet the image of the celebrity superagent is a mystified promise. For working-class African American and Latino students in charters, the image or presence of an Agassi provides no inspiration or model for academic development or the possibilities of learning as a tool for self and social development. If anything, the image of the celebrity attached to the school affirms a bodily and identitarian explanation for why society is the way it is—the truth of racialized poverty and gross inequality is to be found not in the ways historical discourse makes material reality intelligible but rather in the alleged nature of the people in the schools and community. Hence the celebrity image functions as a compact racialized class-based lesson that locates the unequal distribution of life chances in the alleged nature of the student. Just as standardized testing offers an implicit lesson that inequality of opportunity and material resources are the result of a lack of hard work and talent of the student, so too the celebrity image in the school stands as the corporeal proof that financial success is possible and that if the student does not achieve it, only the lone student is to blame.

Smashing the Swindle

I HAVE SHOWN HERE how banks, investors, the rich, and their professional-class implementers have developed a number of resource-skimming schemes under the guise of efficiency, numerical accountability, and cost savings. These schemes, like the 2017 Republican tax law, are an upward redistribution of wealth at the expense of the public.

To counter the swindles of innovative educational finance, citizens must challenge the laws and policies that allow public services to be privatized, sold off, and pillaged. They must comprehend these "innovative" schemes and "public–private partnerships" as similar to vouchers and charters, efforts to replace public sectors with private industries. They must organize and struggle for investment in public goods and services as a condition for a democratic society. However, citizens must also do the crucial cultural work of displacing the language and logic of both markets and radical empiricism and its false faith in decontextualized numbers. Such crucial culture work involves imagining alternatives to accommodation to market imperatives.

A vast amount of educational discourse mistakenly presumes that the solution to the crisis of truth and fact is to get more and better data rather than to examine the assumptions behind the collection of data and the interpretations of what data mean. For example, liberal policy wonks dispute conservatives' use of standardized test scores to advance privatization schemes. Liberal wonks challenge the methodological approach to crunching the data and the numerical outcomes often without addressing the glaringly obvious false assumption that numbers and tests equate to learning. Data cannot drive teaching or leadership. Theoretical assumptions create the conditions within which data become meaningful. In this sense, theory is a crucial instrument for a reflective society. All practices are undergirded by theoretical assumptions. The matter is for people to become more cognizant of what theories, theoretical traditions, assumptions, and ideologies inform their actions. It is crucial for educative institutions at all levels to foster people's capacity to theorize claims to truth as a precondition for democratic agency.

The chapters herein show that a number of educational finance schemes undermine the public interest and drain the public wealth under the guise of innovation and efficiency and through use of market metaphors that are grounded more in faith than in evidence. There are, however, a number of avenues by which educators, cultural producers, and public-minded citizens can fight back. One way to respond to these schemes is to reject them through electoral politics and to put pressure on legislators and policy makers. Another form of resistance is through activism and movements that link the growing public demands among teachers and their unions for fair pay and work conditions to an overt rejection of the onslaught of educational privatization in its more evident forms, such as charters, vouchers, and tax credits, and also in its more stealth forms, such as finance schemes. For example, progressive teacher unions like the Chicago Teachers Union Caucus of Rank and File Educators have explicitly linked their defense of teacher work and public schools to the criticism of neoliberal educational restructuring and broader systemic struggles over class, race, and politics. Struggles around the world, including in Chile and Quebec, have linked fights for local conditions to a broader struggle for the defense of public education as a precondition for democratic society. Those struggling for public and democratic forms of ownership and control of cultural institutions fight against privatized ownership and concentrated control. As the chapters here illustrated, increasingly, the efforts of privatizers aim to displace the physical school and the bodies of teachers. As rightist think tanks imagine replacing physical schools with "unbundled" pay-for-fee services and online education, technology companies replace flesh-and-blood teachers with software and hardware, centralizing, standardizing, and homogenizing curricular and pedagogical decisions. Meanwhile, teachers and students increasingly take a stand putting their bodies on the line in the street and in other public spaces to demand public investment in public education and other humane values. Efforts against the "accountability" standardized testing movement, such as the Opt Out movement, ought to be linked to the rejection of various forms of educational privatization, including adaptive learning and so-called personalized learning technologies. Moreover, these struggles need to comprehend that the problem of standardized testing and the privatization schemes selling it is the same problem of "fake news" and the guise of disinterested objectivity in journalism and politics—a problem of the positivist legacy and the alienation of fact. There needs to be a crucial educative dimension to these movement struggles that pushes back against the false assurances of foundational truth in numbers and bodies and against the false faith in markets.

Electoral politics and activism are necessary but insufficient parts of what needs to grow as a global movement to expand public and critical forms of education against the onslaught of privatization, corporate culture, and other manifestations of neoliberal education and culture. Educators and cultural producers are always in a position to make meanings, produce identifications, and create subject positions. Pedagogical projects can provide students with the intellectual tools and traditions of thought to criticize antidemocratic and antipublic schemes and to imagine radically just and emancipatory futures. A number of critical theory traditions teach students not only to comprehend what is being done to them but also to move beyond passive and spectatorial forms of agency and cults of personality and become publicly oriented and democratic agents capable of acting collectively to impact and govern with others the world they inhabit.

Kenneth J. Saltman is professor in the Educational Leadership and Policy Studies doctoral program at the University of Massachusetts, Dartmouth. His books include *Scripted Bodies: Corporate Power, Smart Technologies, and the Undoing of Public Education*; *The Politics of Education: A Critical Introduction,* 2nd ed.; *Toward a New Common School Movement*; *Neoliberalism, Education, Terrorism* (with Henry Giroux et al.); *The Failure of Corporate School Reform*; and *The Gift of Education: Venture Philanthropy and Public Education.*